S. A. Martin

The man of Uz

Lessons for Young Christians from the Life on an Ancient Saint

S. A. Martin

The man of Uz
Lessons for Young Christians from the Life on an Ancient Saint

ISBN/EAN: 9783337340896

Printed in Europe, USA, Canada, Australia, Japan

Cover: Foto ©Lupo / pixelio.de

More available books at **www.hansebooks.com**

THE MAN OF UZ.

LESSONS FOR YOUNG CHRISTIANS FROM THE LIFE OF AN ANCIENT SAINT.

BY THE

REV. S. A. MARTIN,

PROFESSOR OF HOMILETICS, LINCOLN UNIVERSITY.

"Behold, the fear of the Lord, that is wisdom."
JOB 28:28.

PHILADELPHIA:
PRESBYTERIAN BOARD OF PUBLICATION
AND SABBATH-SCHOOL WORK,
1334 CHESTNUT STREET.

COPYRIGHT, 1891, BY

THE TRUSTEES OF THE

PRESBYTERIAN BOARD OF PUBLICATION
AND SABBATH-SCHOOL WORK.

All Rights Reserved.

WESTCOTT & THOMSON,
Stereotypers and Electrotypers, Philada.

TO THE

YOUNG PEOPLE'S SOCIETIES OF CHRISTIAN ENDEAVOR

THIS BOOK IS AFFECTIONATELY DEDICATED

AS A TOKEN OF

ADMIRATION AND HOPE.

CONTENTS.

CHAPTER I.
	PAGE
A Gentleman of the Old School	7

CHAPTER II.
| Satan at the Court of Heaven | 22 |

CHAPTER III.
| Satan Let Loose | 36 |

CHAPTER IV.
| The Heroism of Endurance | 50 |

CHAPTER V.
| An Ancient Creed | 67 |

CHAPTER VI.
| Mysterious Providence | 83 |

CHAPTER VII.

THE YOUNG MAN'S VIEWS 104

CHAPTER VIII.

OUT OF THE WHIRLWIND 120

THE MAN OF UZ.

CHAPTER I.

A GENTLEMAN OF THE OLD SCHOOL.

"A perfect and an upright man, one that feareth God and escheweth evil."

NO man knows who wrote the book called Job, or who Job was, or where or when he lived. Of unknown date and authorship, it is the most catholic of books. It is a great world-drama untrammelled by time or place or other accident; it tells of an experience which in all of its essential features might be yours or mine or any man's. It never loses its interest, because it treats of questions that are as old as human history and as common as human tears.

Like some grand oratorio composed by an unknown master, its harmonies resound in every age, sublime and sweet, for they are true to the chords of human feeling.

It is, beyond all doubt, a gem of rarest beauty, and it does not concern us greatly to know who digged it from the mine of truth, who gave to it such literary polish or who fixed it in its sacred setting in the word of God.

We take the book up simply as the book takes up its hero, without a word about his genealogy or race or time or place in history; simply, "There was a man in the land of Uz, whose name was Job," and then proceeding straight away to tell us of his character and his experience.

His character is very briefly but sufficiently described in a single sentence: "He feared God and eschewed evil." This is the root of the matter. If you know what a man fears—that is, holds in reverence and love—you know the main line of his life and thought and action, for out of the heart are the issues of life.

Job was perfect and upright because he feared God and eschewed evil. This was the bed-rock on which he built his character, and because it had this rock foundation it fell not when the floods of tribulation came.

Job's greatness rested chiefly on this: the fear of God. This is the fundamental thought that underlies the whole book. As the fundamental air runs through some great oratorio, never lost even amid the most elaborate and varied harmonies, so in this book we find in all the agonized distress of the bereaved and broken-hearted hero, in all his lofty disquisitions on the magnificence of God's creation and in all his pondering on the mysteries of Providence this simple creed recurring : " Behold the fear of the Lord, that is wisdom ; and to depart from evil is understanding." This was the one thing which Job believed and held to when all else seemed unreliable. This was the one thing which could not be shaken, and which remained when the Lord shook not the earth only, but the very heavens.

What, then, is this "fear of God" which God saw in Job, and, seeing, commended ; which Job clung to with such unwavering faith when all else seemed hopeless ruin ? It was not the dread and terror which spring from a guilty conscience : far from that. It was nothing akin to that fright which evil-doers feel at every thought of a righteous God to whom each one must give account of himself. It was, first of all, an unwavering confidence that God reigneth, and that he doeth all things well. From this conviction flowed that deep and solemn reverence which bows in awe before Him who is clothed with majesty and girded about with might. It was a deep and earnest sense of personal responsibility to a personal and holy God.

This is the kind of fear that lies at the foundation of all noble character. There is no more important truth in all the world than this, that a great, deep, earnest reverence for the realities of life and a profound conviction that God rules is the very first essential of true human greatness. Nothing in the world so certainly and utterly destroys all possibility of wise and graceful manhood as a frivolous and irreverent habit of mind, a flippant, pert and brainless skepticism. There is a kind of doubt that is akin to reverence. It is the serious perplexity of men who search for truth and wisdom; who stand, as Job stood, looking out upon this world, of which the most sublime and awful contents are but a whisper of God's power. They stand astonished at the vastness of life's problems, and confess with Job, "These things are too wonderful for me." This kind of doubt the Lord respects.

But there is a much more common kind of skepticism, which is as far removed from this as hell is from heaven. It is shallow, thoughtless, insincere. Its chief employment is the ridicule of sacred things which great men of every creed and every age meditate upon with awe. It dismisses with a silly joke themes which wise men ponder with reverence and deep humility. It answers with a sneer the counsels of experience and age; and, most contemptible of all, it scoffs at a mother's faith and despises a father's prayers.

The young man who affects the airs of this kind of skepticism, and, with a little smattering of science, less of history and none of philosophy, and an insignificant experience of life in any of its deeper phases, sets up as an oracle and critic, and poses before the mirror of his own conceit as the type and embodiment of progress and advanced thought, is perhaps the most petty and the most utterly contemptible style of fool that now afflicts this weary world.

The utter drivel which these fellows pour upon us from the novel, story, essay or daily editorial is one of the most humiliating proofs that in spite of all our boasting the progress of the world in wisdom is a very slow and tedious matter.

The truth is, man is a very small creature in a very great universe. On every hand we are confronted with problems whose vastness we can but faintly conceive and on whose practical solution the welfare of millions depends. More and more the study of nature and history is revealing the tremendous sweep of principles and laws which are the Fates of modern thought. More and more we realize the truth that the free action of to-day will crystallize over-night and be our destiny to-morrow.

"Lo these are the outskirts of his ways, but how small a whisper do we hear of him; the thunder of his power who can understand?"

All true appreciation of the great and beautiful will lead toward greatness in ourselves. A deep respect for that which *is*, an honest love of truth and hatred of all sham and pretence and lies, is not in itself greatness or goodness, but it is the first step toward both.

This fear of God, this confidence in him who reigneth, this solemn reverence for truth and righteousness, was the distinguishing mark of Job's character on its Godward side. This was the attitude of his soul toward what is high and sacred. The sinward side was the antithesis of this: "He eschewed evil."

The word eschew was formerly the same as shun, and it means nearly the same thing, but is more emphatic. The figure that is in the word is that of a horse "shying" at a dangerous or doubtful object. To eschew evil means not merely to keep from open acts of wickedness, but to shun it, to "shy" at even the suggestion of it. Evil is not a thing to be trifled with. You do not, unless you are a fool, trifle with small-pox or mad dogs or rattlesnakes. It is more dangerous to trifle with sin than with these; you may charm the snake, you may escape the most deadly and contagious disease and be none the worse for the risk you ran, but you cannot come in contact with sin and escape unhurt. You cannot dabble in sin without soiling your soul. It is not a matter of choice, but of necessity; sin is in its very nature a defiling and a deadly thing. The only safe rule is the old rule: "Enter not into the path of the wicked, and go not in the way of evil men. Avoid it, pass not by it, turn from it, and pass away."

This first verse gives us the key to the whole of Job's character. He was perfect because his heart was right with God.

It is ever so: permanently good character can grow only out of a pure and honest heart. We hear much of the influence of "environment," and environment has very much to do with the development of character, as the soil and season have very much to do with the development of the fruit in your garden; but men do not "gather grapes of thorns nor figs of thistles," even in the best of seasons; no more can right affections and right moral principles originate in the environment or circumstances of any man.

Job's environment was favorable. In his circumstances Job was greatly blessed. God had made a hedge about him, and about his house, and about all that he had on every side; he had greatly blessed the work of his hands, and his substance was increased in the land. As it is true that our circumstances have much to do with the forming of our character, so it is true that God by his wise providence determines our circumstances. The point which Satan raised was not whether Job's environment was favorable, for that is admitted, but whether it was not the sole cause of his piety.

Let us see just how much of Job's character was due to his favorable circumstances.

His wealth and high position gave him opportunities of noble conduct which men in humbler circumstances do not have; these opportunities, well improved, became the means of greater grace and higher culture than he could have reached without them. He had been intrusted with many talents, and his faithful use of them gave him just claim to many honors. "To him that hath shall be given." This is the law of nature, as well as of grace. As his goodness made his wealth a blessing, so his wealth gave means of increasing his goodness by doing good. As his prosperity gave lustre to his piety, so his piety gave dignity to his wealth. The expression "poor but pious" is so largely overused that we too often get the impression that success in business and integrity of heart are incompatible; that to be pious one must needs be poor. This is not the teaching of Scripture or of experience. Wealth is a form of power which, if rightly used, may greatly strengthen and develop godliness in character. It is the *love* of money that is a root of all evil; it is the greed of gain that starves the nobler affections of the man; and it is the danger of pride and arrogance growing out of riches that led Agur, like a prudent man, to pray, "Give me neither poverty nor riches." But wealth with grace to use it is a blessing, for it gives opportunities of benefaction and influence for good. It is doubtless easier to be faithful in the use of two talents than in the use of five; but he that was faithful with the five received the greater reward.

Here are some of the ways Job used these talents of wealth:

He did not eat his portion alone, and let the fatherless go hungry.

He did not dwell in his luxury while the poor were without covering. They lodged in his house, and they were warmed with the fleece of his sheep.

He was patient as well as just with his servant, for he said, "the same God made us both;" both were liable to err; both must seek for mercy, and not justice only.

He was not haughty on account of his wealth, nor did he make gold his confidence.

He was "given to hospitality," and gentle to those inferior to him in place and power.

On the other hand, he scorned to seek popularity at the cost of dignity or justice; the adverse criticism and rebukes of his friends could not drive him from his loyalty to his own conscience. I cannot imagine a more complete picture of dignified and noble manhood than this.

But this is not all. He was not only a noble man, a kind neighbor, a generous master and a faithful friend, but also a kind and sympathetic father. We are told that "children are an heritage from God," and there is no more accursed infidelity than the modern unbelief of this.

Job's family is mentioned first, as chiefest of his blessings, and so he seems to have regarded them. He mentions it as one of the joys of his prosperous days that his children were about him. And they were not only about him, but they seem to have been a congenial family. The fact that they went and feasted in each other's houses is not a matter of much importance in itself, but it is doubtless mentioned because of what it implies. It implies harmony and good-will. "Behold how good and how pleasant it is for brethren to dwell together in unity." Still more is implied in the fact that they sent for their sisters to eat and drink with them. The presence of ladies is mostly a good guarantee that a feast will not be a drunken revel, and the presence of our sisters is never asked when we have anything on hand that we are ashamed of. There is no better test than this. It is a very bad sign when a young man does not want his sisters present where he wants to go himself. Any place of entertainment where you do not wish to see your sister is no fit place for you. It is not said that Job took part in these festivities himself, but he seems to have given considerable thought to them. The care he exercised over the spiritual welfare of his sons is the most beautiful evidence of his own piety. A good man will make his children's welfare, especially their spiritual welfare, his first consideration. We cannot bequeath our piety as a legacy to our children; we cannot regenerate them; but we can do a great deal to shield them from temptation and to develop in them sound manly principles by bringing them up in a clean and wholesome moral atmosphere; and no considerations of business or ambition can justify us in taking risks in a matter so vital as the welfare of our own children. Alas, that any one should need exhortation to this duty! but the utter recklessness with which men, in pursuit of gain, take their sons and daughters into the most dangerous influences, at the time of life when character most easily receives impressions from without, is one of the most crying evils of the day. Job was thoughtful for his children. He had reason for good hopes concerning them, but that was not enough to satisfy a faithful father; he provides, as far as he can, against the possibility of evil. "And it was so, when the days of their feasting were gone about, that Job sent and sanctified them, and rose up early in the morning, and offered burnt offerings according to the number of them all: for Job said, It may be that my sons have sinned, and cursed God in their hearts. Thus did Job continually."

Here is an admirable practicable treatment of a problem that has occupied the mind of every thoughtful parent from Job's day to ours—namely, How shall our children have good times and not be the worse for it? We all know that gay rounds of festive pleasures, even though they be the most innocent attainable, have a very strong tendency to crowd out serious thoughts and sadly interfere with spiritual growth.

Job met the case this way: he did not say, "There is danger in all such festivities; my sons must therefore give them up;" nor did he say, with careless tone, "Oh, let them go while they are young; they will grow old and sober soon enough." I believe the devil invented that saying. No; he kept in fullest sympathy with them in their festivity, but took good care, in due time, to turn their minds again to serious things. He did not intrude the solemn exercises of religious worship on their hours of amusement—there is a time for all things—but when the feasting was over the good father called them to serious thoughts and the solemn service of religious worship.

There is a time to laugh and a time to pray, and a little more thoughtfulness and consideration for the fitness of times and places would make our laugh more merry and our prayers more fervent, to the great improvement of them both.

Job used the ordinances of his time; he offered a special sacrifice for each one of his children. This he did continually, and was commended for so doing. There are men now who would say to Job, "You make a great mistake; any religious service performed in that habitual way is likely to become a mere formality; see what a perfunctory matter family worship becomes when made a part of the daily routine of duty!" But Job was not the kind of man to be deceived by any such plausible nonsense. He knew from his own experience that regular and stated times for religious service is a matter of great importance. Nothing is well done when left to mere impulse and convenience. When we become irregular in our attendance on the means of grace, public, social or private, we are already in poor health spiritually. The man who has a good appetite was never yet heard to complain of the monotony of three regular meals each day.

"Rejoice, O young man, in thy youth, ... but remember," says the wise man. Remember that just beyond the days of youth there are days of manhood, days that will call for all your strength and wisdom, days that are full of opportunities of all true greatness. You will need all the sacred influences you can have to fit you well for those

A GENTLEMAN OF THE OLD SCHOOL. 21

good days. Then there is above all this, beyond the things that are seen and temporal, the region of eternal verity, a personal God of infinite majesty and love. He has a plan and purpose for you, a destiny right glorious and excellent. Remember, O young man, remember this.

"The best is yet to be
    The last of life, for which the first was made:
  Our times are in His hand
  Who saith, 'A *whole* I planned;
    Youth shows but half; trust God: see all, nor be afraid."

CHAPTER II.

SATAN AT THE COURT OF HEAVEN.

"Now there was a day when the sons of God came to present themselves before the Lord, and Satan came also among them."

THE word "Satan" signifies the adversary. The evil spirit to whom this name is given is preeminently the one adverse to man. He is adverse to every human interest. He is the arch-enemy, the seducer and traducer of our race and of each soul. He was a murderer from the beginning, and abode not in the truth. We are therefore shocked to find him here presenting himself at the court of Heaven among the sons of God. And not only does he come into the presence of the Lord, but he presents himself as one who has some right to come. There is an assurance about his manner that seems to imply a certain claim to recognition. He reports his "going to and fro in the earth, and walking up and down in it" as if it were an employment allowed, if not assigned to him. The Lord talks with him concerning Job as a king might talk with his minister concerning the affairs of a province. But it seems still more surprising to find that the Lord gives him permission to go and exercise all his malignant powers against the man who "feared God and eschewed evil." He is allowed to strip Job of all that he possessed, and afterward his license is extended that he might afflict him in body and mind, forbidden only to take his life. It is indeed startling to read that "the Lord said unto Satan, Behold, he is in thine hand; but save his life." The Lord puts a perfect and an upright man into the hands of the arch-enemy, to be afflicted, tormented and abused to the utmost limit of living endurance.

This representation of Satan and his relation to God is sometimes explained as being the imperfect conception of the author of this ancient book. We are told that the doctrines of demonology were not fully developed at the time this book was written, and that we have to read what is here represented in the fuller, clearer light of the teaching of the New Testament. We are warned to be careful not to impose on Job the conceptions belonging to a later and more advanced period. All this is true in a sense, but rather misleading. It is doubtless true that the New Testament gives fuller knowledge on this, as on all other doctrines, than is given in the Old Testament; but, on the other hand, it is true that nowhere in Scripture do we have so complete a picture of Satan and of his relations to God as we have here. Nor do we anywhere find his "great might and deep guile" so clearly revealed.

We have no right to say that an author's knowledge is imperfect if all that he has any occasion to say is accurately said. It would be folly to argue that because a man has written a history of Asia therefore he knows nothing of Europe. It is equal folly to conclude that the author of the book of Job held imperfect notions of Satan because he does not mention all that we find in later books. A good deal of what we are told of the development of doctrine is of this sort.

The fact that excites remark here is that Satan is represented as the servant rather than the enemy of God. He has access to his presence; he brings an accusation against a saint, and receives permission to afflict him, so that it can be said with equal truth that "Satan smote Job," or "the Lord hath taken away."

This strikes us as remarkable; but the author of this book sees nothing remarkable in it; at least, he states it as the most natural thing in the world.

We are surprised because we have not thought very deeply about it. Our surprise will disappear, if I mistake not, when we ask ourselves, What else can Satan be but the servant of God? If God be omnipotent and sovereign, Satan cannot act but by his high permission. The notion of an eternal principle or power of evil warring against the good is utterly foreign to Scripture, old or new. It may seem strange, but it is certainly true, that Satan is as dependent on God as we are. Neither man nor devil lives one moment but by God's all-animating breath.

Satan comes into God's presence because he can do nothing else : there is no corner in this vast universe where he may hide from his sovereign, no realm where he may dwell and be forgotten. He must say, even as we say, "Whither shall I go from thy spirit? or whither shall I flee from thy presence? If I ascend up into heaven, thou art there; if I make my bed in hell, behold, thou art there."

But we are told that this appearance of Satan at the court of Heaven is merely a dramatic figure, a poetic image not to be taken literally. Of course this is poetry, and of course it is not to be taken literally ; but it is not any the less strictly accurate as a statement of truth. We are no more at liberty to reject the teaching of poetry than we are to reject that of prose. The habit of reading into the words of Scripture any meaning which those words are capable of conveying in any circumstances is a common but deplorable means of falsifying Scripture. When Christ said, "I am the vine, ye are the branches," he taught a wonderful truth just as distinctly as when he said, "If ye love me, keep my commandments." And we have no more right to shift the meaning of the one passage than we have to reject the teaching of the other.

The essential matter here is briefly this: God is Sovereign; Satan may not touch Job, nor the least of his possessions, without distinct permission from the Lord. He may afflict and tempt and harass the children of men, but only so far as God's good purposes allow. This representation of Satan's relation to God is not only in harmony with the latest revelation that we have on the subject, but it is the latest; we have nothing beyond this.

But Satan, though the servant of God, is none the less Satan—the adversary. The charge which he brings against Job has three marks of Satanic origin: it is false, it is malignant, it is cynical. "He is a liar from the beginning and the father of it." He is wonderfully skillful in the use of all the vile arts of falsehood, deceit and insincerity. It is well to know the marks of Satan's authorship, as it is well to know the marks of poisonous weeds and deadly serpents. The "higher criticism" that will teach us all to recognize the hand of Satan in what we read and hear will be a useful science.

His lies are very plausible; they much resemble truth, and have moreover a show of shrewdness. They are skillfully compounded, containing a fair amount of pleasant truth and but one drop of the poison of error, but that poison is deadly. The first lie that ever defiled the air of Paradise was his assertion to our first parents in the garden of Eden. "Ye shall not surely die," said he, "for God doth know that in the day ye eat thereof, then shall your eyes be opened, and ye shall be as gods, knowing good and evil." And mankind has found, when too late, that the deadly falsehood lay in words that were, in one sense, true: their eyes were opened; they did indeed know good and evil. Alas, the evil we have known from that first disobedience! We, whom God would have to know but good, know evil much more intimately; not as the gods, but as the devils know it. To our Saviour the Tempter quotes Scripture with the same subtle plausibility. So here, in the very court of Heaven, he brings an accusation against God's servant with such an appearance of shrewd insight into character that men who pride themselves on their superior knowledge of mankind repeat it as a maxim of their political philosophy in the phrase, " Every man has his price." Satan said, "Doth Job fear God for nought? Hast not thou made a hedge about him, and about his house, and about all that he hath on every side? Thou hast blessed the work of his hands, and his substance is increased in the land. But put forth thine hand now, and touch all that he hath, and he will curse thee to thy face." How plausible it sounds! how often we hear it, almost word for word, from the bitter lips of cynical and sneering critics who boast of their keen insight into the secret motives of the human heart! But it is the devil's doctrine; it has the trail of the serpent upon it for ever.

Men say, "There is a good deal of truth in it." Certainly there is; there is much truth in all of Satan's lies. He is the most expert and crafty of liars. He is no such unskilled novice in the art of deception as to offer us that which does not even look like truth. A counterfeit coin is dangerous just in proportion to its close resemblance to the genuine; so every lie must wear a mask of truth or no one is deceived.

Satan does not say that Job is a hypocrite: that was a coarse and clumsy charge brought by his angry friends. Satan is much more subtle and malignant: he admits the facts, but impugns his motives. He does not question the statement that Job is perfect and upright so far as conduct is concerned, but he attributes it all to selfishness. He seems to say, and to sneer as he says it, "True, Job does well, very well indeed, and he would be a great fool to do anything else; what could he do that will pay him as well as this piety? It is, I fancy, rather easy to be pious on his income, and whatever sacrifice he makes is very well rewarded. Even a dog will fawn upon the hand that feeds him. Job is pious for profit; stop his wages, and you will see that it is so; he will renounce you openly." Such was Satan's first accusation. God, for some good purpose, gives him permission to put Job to the test. Calamity after calamity falls upon him, till he is stripped of all he owned and bereft of all his children; unmerciful disaster pursues him, like unrelenting fate, till he is childless, penniless and forsaken, naked as when he was born.

But the adversary is foiled. "Job arose, and

rent his mantle, and shaved his head, and fell down upon the ground, and worshiped, and said, Naked came I out of my mother's womb, and naked shall I return thither: the Lord gave, and the Lord hath taken away; blessed be the name of the Lord."

Such a test would seem sufficient, but Satan's malice is insatiable. His hatred of the perfect man is only inflamed by the proof of his integrity. Again he appears in the court of Heaven, not to confess defeat and ask forgiveness for his abuse of Job: far from that. He comes to repeat his accusation and to ask for license to afflict and torture Job still further. With devilish ingenuity he argues that the test he was permitted to make was quite inadequate to the case; it did not touch Job close enough; the root of his selfish service was not reached, could not be reached, without striking Job himself. "Skin for skin, yea, all that a man hath will he give for his life." He seems to urge that Job is still enduring in hope of reward. True, he has lost all, but he knows that God is able to give him greater things again. In short, Job is patient now for reward, just as he was pious for reward before; destroy that hope, and then we will have a true test; then we will see, as I said before, that he will renounce you openly. Such was the final accusation which the adversary laid against this ancient saint in the court of Heaven. How plausible it is! "His hidden craft is matchless."

It is true that Job will lose nothing by his patient faith. "God is a rewarder of them that diligently seek him." How then can it be proved that godliness is ever anything more than enlightened selfishness? How, indeed, but by proof-test? This is, therefore, a subtle defamation of all piety and godliness; one that has been repeated by devilish tongues in every age. But it is even more than this: it is an impious challenge against God himself. It amounts to this, that there is no such thing as sincere, disinterested goodness in the world—that even God's love and kindness can inspire in man nothing higher than a mercenary allegiance. If Satan is right, if "every man has his price," and selfishness is the fundamental ruling principle in all men, then there is no real virtue in the world, and God's effort to win our devotion and our love is a failure.

If this were only a question of Job's integrity, or of the integrity of any one man, it would be of comparatively little importance. But it is a living question. The devil and his agents have not ceased to teach this doctrine, and many a poor soul is ensnared by this device. It is a common thing to hear men try to palliate, if not excuse, their selfishness by this Satanic cry, "All men are just the same." So powerful is the tendency to measure our own righteousness by the character of our neighbor that nothing will so soon corrupt the conscience and make a man ready to be dishonest as the belief that others are dishonest also. No doctrine is more thoroughly devilish and full of mischief than the teaching that all virtue is sham, all honesty mere policy and all piety hypocrisy. This doctrine is the more dangerous because there is so much apparent truth in it. There is so much sham and insincerity in the world that we are often ready in our haste to say, as David said in his haste, "All men are liars." But it is to the honor of humanity that it can be said that this accusation of Satan against humanity is false. Not only did Job prove that there is, in some men at least, a noble devotion to righteousness that is stronger than the love of self, but history is full of evidence against this doctrine of the devil. Many a man has given up his life rather than his honor; many have died rather than be cowards or traitors. The martyrs, that noble army whom the whole world delights to honor,—what are they but witnesses, living witnesses, in heaven, testifying by their very presence there that there have been multitudes to whom life was sweet, but duty sweeter? The common excuse for sin, that "a man must live," is the whine of the coward and the shirk; men, true men, in every age have scorned to put honor in the balance against life. Their motto is, "Quit you like men, be strong."

But if we would know how false Satan's estimate of man is, we may compare it with the estimate which was put on us by Him who "knew what was in man." Satan says man is thoroughly and supremely selfish; pay him well enough and he will be pious as you wish; but he has his price; honor and virtue and loyalty are always in the market; they can all be bought if you pay enough.

This picture of us is like a skillfully drawn caricature: it has so strong a resemblance to the truth that we may not be able to say where the false lines are, but that it is not true becomes evident the moment we bring it side by side with the true portrait drawn by the Master. Then we see that it is totally and meanly false. The meek and lowly Man of Nazareth knows man better, infinitely better, than the sneering fiend, and yet Jesus of

Nazareth thought man was worth redeeming with his own divine blood. None know so well as he the sad depths to which we have fallen, but in his pity there is no contempt; in all his rebukes there is never a sneer. He who created us in the image of God saw the traces of that image even in the publicans and harlots to whom he brought the gospel of forgiveness and hope. You remember Elijah's cry of despair, "I only am left," and God's reply, "I have seven thousand in Israel."

You remember also the command of Christ to begin the preaching of the gospel in Jerusalem. All worldly wisdom would say, "That is a great mistake. Better go to some place where the people are not so violently prejudiced against the gospel; it is certain that these people of Jerusalem will never turn to Christ." Nevertheless the command was given, the gospel of remission of sins was preached in prejudiced Jerusalem, and, to our amazement, a great cry is heard on the lips of thousands, "What shall we do?" and there were added to the Church about three thousand souls in a single day.

Pessimism is of the devil; to grow discouraged is human. Jesus Christ has given us a gospel of abounding hope, a hope that maketh not ashamed.

May he open our eyes to see in every man a soul that Christ loves and for whom Christ died. To bring accusations against our race is Satan's work, not ours. To believe them is to put Satan's estimate above Christ's. It may be that some of our hopes shall fail, and that some of those we trust will disappoint us, but on the whole God will do exceedingly above all that we ask or think. He who works with the largest hope will work with the stoutest heart, and will see most of his hopes realized.

"He prayeth best who loveth best
All things both great and small;
For the dear God that loveth us,
He made and loveth all."

CHAPTER III.

SATAN LET LOOSE.

"So went Satan forth from the presence of the Lord, and smote Job."

CHARLES KINGSLEY once remarked that "Satan's latest trick is to pretend that he is dead." A much older theologian observed that it has always been a favorite device with the Evil One to persuade men that he does not exist. If this be his design, he has much reason to exult in its success, for while there are few who go so far as openly to deny the fact of his existence, there are multitudes to whom he is practically nothing more than a dead devil. There are, indeed, very few who have any adequate conception of his real presence and power on the earth.

The fact of a powerful spirit, full of all malice, constantly active to destroy us is scarcely felt at all as one of the factors of human affairs. It is a very poor general who fails to learn all that may be known of the enemy's character and power and designs; so he is but an ill-trained soldier of Jesus Christ who neglects the information God has given us concerning the great enemy of our souls. We will well deserve defeat if we are so foolish as to accept without consideration the mere rumors of the camp concerning Satan and his devices, especially when these rumors bear the most suspicious marks of Satan's authorship. The present popular notions of the Evil One are just such as favor his design of concealment, and thus give him easy access to the citadel of our hearts.

The most popular conceptions of Satan at this time are wonderfully ill-considered and often grossly absurd. A few of the more common of these notions may be classified and examined under three general forms, one or other of which they generally assume:

The first we may call the transcendental theory. This represents Satan as a philosophical abstraction signifying evil influences in general. He is, according to this theory, the personification of the hurtful, the corrupting, the degrading; in short, of every influence that makes for unrighteousness. This doctrine is put forward under banners most likely to attract the eye and win the popular favor. It is introduced as " advanced," " modern," " scientific" and whatever else may serve to advertise it as something new and different from the traditional faith. The chief reason for its being accepted lies in the reaction that has followed the too vivid fancy concerning Satan's personal agency in the affairs of men. The witchcraft craze of the seventeenth century, with its barbarity and shame, was not only the death-struggle of a degrading superstition, but it was also the beginning of a reaction which has carried the present age far to the opposite extreme. Because the absurd garments in which the ignorant fancy of the Middle Ages had clothed Satan have been cast out of respectable belief we deceive ourselves with the notion that we have got rid of the fiend himself. This doctrine of Satan is, however, never received on its own merits. It comes in as a part of a whole system of theology, which strives to retain old names and forms of doctrine, but interprets out of them all positive meaning, leaving little more than a lot of pretty allegories which may mean this or that or nothing, according to the reader's fancy.

Of course, such a doctrine is practically a mere denial that any such person as Satan exists, and it is all the more dangerous because it does not shock our conservative sense by saying so too plainly. It is the most subtle form of Satan's design to persuade men that he does not exist.

The second form of popular conception of Satan we may call the mediæval. This represents him as a grotesque and absurd but not very dangerous being. He is pictured as horned and hoofed, armed with a pitchfork, the coarse companion of witches, cowardly, cunning and superstitious. This is the devil of the common theatre and of pictorial art. It is the popular conception of the ignorant and the worldly. In the minds of such, Satan is associated with the spectacular drama, blue-fire and a smell of brimstone. His name suggests to them the comedian and the property-room of the theatre, rather than any serious reality of the moral world. This notion of the Evil One is the result of Middle Age superstition worked over by modern irreverence. The state of mind in which it flourishes is that which finds amusement in irreverent remarks on sacred things and fancies that they are witty. In the minds of the rude and ignorant this conception answers Satan's purpose quite as well as the transcendental view does in the minds of the more cultured. In both his object is to conceal his deadly malice and great might and to persuade men that he does not exist. In the one case he is merely a subjective image, a figment of the imagination, denoting certain more or less real evils, but devoid of personality, and therefore not to be dreaded as a present danger. In the other conception of him there is such an air of absurdity, of "bouffe," such a flavor of unreality and buffoonery, that it is almost impossible to persuade any one to take him seriously. It is evident that, whether he originated these notions of himself or not, they are exceedingly well suited to his subtle purpose of pretending he is dead.

There is a third conception of Satan's character, which we may call the heroic. This presents him as the unsuccessful but brilliant leader of a great rebellion in heaven. He is wicked but magnificent. John Milton's poetic genius created this picture for us, and, Puritan though he was, he has made the Satan of "Paradise Lost" one of the most interesting characters in all literature. Milton does not fail to tell us that Satan is bad, but at the same time he exhibits in him such bravery and fortitude, such shrewdness, skill and eloquence, that we cannot but admire him, and while our judgment is against him our sympathies are with him. Of course, this is poetry, not dogmatics, but it has for that very reason entered the more widely into the current conceptions of the prince of darkness. Milton was one of the few poets whom the Puritans would read, and his influence must have been very great and very dangerous. It is indeed rather surprising that among all the forms of ungodliness that have been organized or formulated some party has not taken Milton's Satan as their hero and patron. It would be hard to imagine a leader better suited to gain the applause and command the obedience of some anarchist parties, and the time may come when they will read good literature enough to find him. The danger of such a view of Satan's character is evidently of quite another kind from those we have mentioned above. The danger here is not that we come to think of him as unreal, but, believing that he does exist, come to regard him as having a good deal to claim in his favor. Our sympathy so naturally inclines to the weaker party in the conflict that if Satan can be supposed to have any such good qualities as Milton gives him, there will be plenty of silly folk to profess, and possibly to feel, some sentimental admiration for him, just as there are always some weakminded sentimentalists to make heroes of the vilest criminals when they are about to be punished. Sympathy is a lovely grace, but such diseased and morbid sympathy as this, which would turn loose upon society the cruel and brutal wretches whom justice claims for the gallows, is a pitiable kind of idiocy. And yet this is almost wisdom compared to the insanity that would make a hero of the prince of darkness, the malignant enemy of souls.

The Satan of the book of Job is a very different being from any of these. He is an actual, personal, powerful being, shrewd, busy and full of deadly malice. He knows Job thoroughly, and all his circumstances intimately. He hates him with a bitter and aggressive hatred, a hatred that is wholly malignant. Job had done nothing against him on account of which Satan might be expected to hate him. His guile was not

"Stirred up with envy and revenge,"

as Milton puts it; it is the outgoing of native malevolence. It is a bitter and implacable hatred, that knows no reason, no pity, no remorse. It is hatred absolute, malevolence unmixed. It is not rage nor fury nor anger such as mortals know, but black, cold, hellish hate. This is what we have to fight, "For our wrestling is not against flesh and blood, but against the principalities, against the powers, against the world-rulers of this darkness, against the spiritual hosts of wickedness in the heavenly places."

> "Our old, mortal foe
> Now aims his fell blow,
> Great might and deep guile
> His horrid coat-of-mail;
> On earth is no one like him."

He comes forth from the presence of the Lord exulting in his license to hurt Job and gloating over the prospect of seducing him from his integrity. With what eagerness he strikes him! and what weapons he has! The wind and the lightning and the rapacity of man are wielded by him as if they were his own proper weapons. Whether he has power over the forces of nature different in kind from the power man has over the same is an open question. On the one hand, there is no reason to doubt that he may have; on the other hand, there is no necessity for insisting that he has. His superior knowledge of the laws of nature may be quite enough to account for all the facts. Man can do wonders with the lightning now which a very few years ago would have been thought possible only to supernatural beings. That he has power to stir up the minds of wicked men to evil deeds is more certain. Every evil habit, every unrighteous desire is a handle for Satan to hold us by and to lead us captive at his will. There is nothing very mysterious about this. We are familiar with the way by which wicked men influence other men by their vices and evil desires; how they excite them and develop them until they become stronger than conscience, and then pander to them at their own price. The liquor-seller who deliberately creates or intensifies the appetite to which he caters is a horrible example of this devilish method of leading men by the handles of vice. What such men do in their measure Satan does in his larger way. In this, as in other ways which we have noticed, the prince of darkness hides his hand, persuades men that he does not exist. Personal liberty is to men a delusion; to Satan it is a ghastly joke, at which he and the fiends of hell laugh with that horrible laughter which is the mockery of mirth. The father of lies has never circulated a belief that is more intensely false than this, that he is the patron of the bright and joyous side of life. He offers us the gratification of our desires in the name of freedom, but he takes good care that each indulgence makes it harder to abstain, and when desire becomes stronger than principle we are like a ship that has lost its rudder—the wreck is sure to come, no matter what wind blows, for there are dangers on every side. It is just here that we see the insufficiency of all reforms that aim at anything less than a radical change of principle. Little does the Evil One care into which of his traps you fall. What gain is it to escape the snare of drunkenness only to fall into the pit of filthy lewdness? What advantage has the man whose avarice destroys him over the man whose sensuality destroys him? Sometimes it suits the devil's purpose best to have us rich in this world's goods; in other cases it is his aim to take away these things. His attack on Job was by stripping him of all he valued. But his attack on you may be just the opposite. We know not which is the more severe, but we see enough of the danger of both to feel the wisdom of the prayer of Agur, the son of Jakeh, "Give me neither poverty nor riches; feed me with food convenient for me: lest I be full and deny thee, and say, Who is the Lord? or lest I be poor and steal, and take the name of God in vain." All honor to the rich man who is a faithful steward of the good things God has committed to his care, but equal honor to the poor man who is faithful and contented in his lot.

Now see this pretended friend of pleasure, this

patron of happiness, this jolly good fellow, as he would have us believe,—see him when he gets a man in his power. How he hurls his weapons, with scowling hate, till he sees him swept bare of every possession, bereft of every earthly comfort, ruined in fortune and distressed in mind, the object of the pity and compassion of every one who reads his sad story! Surely this is enough to satisfy the spite of even a devil; surely, we say, unprovoked dislike cannot go beyond this. But we are mistaken; here is a hatred that does not know what pity is. He has begged for further license against Job, and, having gotten it, he proceeds to strike the man who is down. He leaps on him, torments him, and uses every means in his power to destroy him, soul and body.

The whole story of Satan's abuse of Job is a picture of the lowest, meanest malice. There is nothing here of the grotesque, the jesting devil of the modern stage or the daily paper. There is nothing here of the heroic Satan of Milton, nor of the vague abstraction of our "progressive" friends. There is nothing here but bitter hatred, implacable, deadly and inhuman. It is the work of the Old Serpent, the horrible Dragon of the bottomless pit.

So it ever is. Our adversary is full of guile; he can assume the appearance of an angel of light; he can pose as the friend of youthful sport, the champion of freedom, the patron of sweetness and light. But look at his victims: are they peaceful? are they joyous? They laugh, perhaps, but it is either with that silly laugh that is like "the crackling of thorns under a pot" or that horrible bar-room laugh that can hardly be distinguished from a curse.

Hardly anything is more indicative of character than the laugh. A terrible history of a soul's degradation might be written by simply describing the laugh—if this were possible—from the silly laugh of those who trifle with sin to the coarse yell of those whom sin has brutalized. Nothing can be farther from mirth than the heart that the Evil One has conquered. It is unspeakably sad, not merely with the sadness of misfortune and pain and disappointment, but with a deeper and darker sadness—a sadness that is not only dark but hideous, terrifying, causing one to shriek with terror.

But Satan is not supreme. He is superhuman, superior to flesh and blood, but the "seed of the woman" hath bruised the serpent's head.

"By might of ours can nought be done:
  Our fate were soon decided.
But for us fights a champion,
  By God himself provided.
Who is this, ask ye?
Jesus Christ: 'tis he:
Lord of Sabaoth,
True God and Saviour both,
  Omnipotent in battle."

So Luther puts it, and so it is. No man can cope with such an adversary. But help hath been laid on one who is mighty to save. He hath taken our nature and become man, that through death he might destroy him that had the power of death, that is, the devil. The more we realize the terrible danger we are in from the great enemy of souls, the more we will feel the need of a divine Saviour to come with the omnipotence of God for our deliverance; the more we will rejoice in the gospel of Christ our Champion and the Captain of our salvation. Then we can sing in triumph,

"Did devils fill the earth and air,
  All eager to devour us,
Our steadfast hearts need feel no care,
  Lest they should overpower us.
The grim prince of hell,
With rage though he swell,

SATAN LET LOOSE.

Hurts us not a whit,
Because his doom is writ;
  A little word can rout him.

"The Word of God will never yield
  To any creature living;
He stands with us upon the field,
  His grace and Spirit giving.
Take they child and wife,
Goods, name, fame and life,—
Though all this be done,
Yet have they nothing won:
  The kingdom still remaineth."*

* ("Ein feste Burg." Trans. of Dr. T. C. Porter.)

CHAPTER IV.

THE HEROISM OF ENDURANCE.

"Ye have heard of the patience of Job."—Jas. 5 : 11.

THE name of Job has become the very synonym of patience. But patience, like the book of Job, must be well known to be appreciated at its proper worth. It is the crowning grace of Christian character, the sweetest and fairest fruit of the Spirit, but its very nature is to hide from sight and observation. The perfection of its beauty consists in this, that it is never showy, but modest, unobtrusive, quiet.

We are prone to estimate all things by the force they show, by the active energy they manifest. We say the blacksmith shapes the iron with his hammer, while the anvil, which outwears a score of hammers, is not so much as mentioned. We speak of the power of steam as that which drives the engine, till, now and then, an explosion reminds us that the strength of resistance must be greater than the force of steam or there will be trouble. So it is in Christian character: the active virtues, such as courage, benevolence, hospitality and the like, are so much more easily seen that we too often come to regard the passive graces, such as meekness, gentleness and patience, as secondary both in beauty and influence; but this is by no means the case. They are not only the eminently Christ-like graces, but they are abundantly fruitful and effective in good works and well-rounded manhood.

The tendency of our religious life to-day is strongly toward the active and utilitarian extreme. To feed the hungry, clothe the naked, nurse the sick, preach the gospel to the poor and send it to the heathen are duties recognized and performed in this age as never before on earth. This is well: we thank God that it is so; but there is a very serious danger that we come to look on these activities as constituting our religion. We need to cultivate with greater care the passive virtues, the graces of endurance, or our life will grow one-sided, lacking symmetry, thus failing of the standard set for us in the gospel, "That ye may stand perfect and complete in all the will of God."

Another difficulty in the way of properly appreciating the grace of patience is that its exercise is so closely connected with what we call our temper, a most uncertain thing in most of us. In some moods we are able to bear much, while in other moods the merest trifles make the currents of our soul run rough and muddy. A piece of iron may be tested and warranted to stand a certain strain at any time, but it is not so with men; at one time we can bear a mountain of outrage or injustice, at another time the grasshopper is a burden. To at all appreciate a test of character in the grace of patience we must consider delicately every circumstance of the trial, and especially the order of the events. It would be hard to imagine circumstances or an order of events better adapted to the devilish purpose of breaking down the patience of a man than that which Satan devised to ruin Job.

Misfortune, affliction, bereavement, pain and dishonor are poured upon him. First, he is stripped of his wealth; then, at one dreadful stroke, his sons and daughters all are taken from him. He was thus, in a moment, dashed from the highest place of fortune to the lowest depth of adversity; he was penniless and desolate. He called his servant and received no answer; he realizes by this that he is deserted. He looked to his wife for sympathy, but she, poor soul! had broken down under these sad losses, and, saddest of all, had lost her faith in God. Job is urged to embrace despair and infidelity. He longs for sympathy, but the very children in the street mock him; there is "none so poor to do him reverence." Such was the order and severity of Satan's first attack. It was devilish in plot and execution, but it failed to shake the faith of the man who "feared God and eschewed evil." "The Lord gave, and the Lord hath taken away; blessed be the name of the Lord," said Job, and the blessed God looked down from heaven on his brave saint with admiration and commendation.

Now the second onset of Satan begins. He strikes Job suddenly with painful and loathsome disease. So sorely is he stricken that he becomes offensive to his own senses, and groans in agony of pain. He cries out in anguish for death to come to his relief. Still he rules his spirit, and from these depths cries unto the Lord with unwavering faith; his soul "waited for the Lord more than they that watch for the morning."

But the end is not yet; there is a severer test awaiting Job, in a quarter where he least expected it. The sharpest trial of his patience comes from his friends. This seems strange, but it is often so: no enemy can so exasperate us as an unreasonable friend. When Job's three friends heard of his affliction and the sad plight he was in, they came at once to see him; with delicate good taste they would not intrude upon his silent grief, but with rent mantles and dust-besprinkled heads they "sat down with him on the ground seven days and seven nights, and none spake a word unto him, for they saw that his grief was very great." This was very kind; it was the first bit of bright sky Job had seen since the storm of trouble burst upon him. But it was only such brightness as Satan always gives when he is managing—a deceitful glimmer only to excite a hope which will soon be quenched and leave him in deeper darkness than before. Satan used these friends for his malignant purposes with great adroitness. They were not turned against Job at once; it might have been easier for Job to bear it if it had been so. It would have saddened his life more, perhaps, but it would not have been so trying to his patience as their wrong-headed friendship was.

They were men of strict integrity; they were sincere friends of Job; they loved him dearly and were deeply grieved in his affliction, all the more because they believed that he had brought it on himself by some sin, which, though hidden from them and from the world, God saw and was now visiting with his displeasure.

Job loved his friends, and strove with all his might to vindicate his character in their sight. But they were men of a settled theory, not open to conviction, probably holding it impious to entertain a doubt of the truth of their creed. "Suffering," they said, "is the penalty of sin; Job suffers, therefore Job has sinned." Moreover, since he suffers so terribly, he must have sinned greatly; the fact that he has seemed good only aggravates the case, for it proves that he was a cunning hypocrite. This was their theology; not wholly false, yet totally misleading; not open to argument, and therefore not to be shaken by facts or logic. Yet these men were by no means stupid bigots. Their manners were courteous and refined, their language dignified and their reasoning high and scholarly. They were gentlemen of a fine type.

Their fault was a fault most prevalent among scholars everywhere—too much confidence in their own opinion. They set themselves to this unpleasant task of bringing Job to penitence and confession, not from any envious pleasure in seeing him humbled, but because they honestly loved him and thoroughly believed that unless he would repent and put away the secret sin, whatever it was, that had brought him to his present sad state, he would be undone for ever. So they come to comfort and to help him.

For one whole week they sit beside him in silent sympathy. "The heart knoweth its own bitterness: and a stranger doth not intermeddle with its joy." They show by every conventional sign of their time and country how they desire to share his burden, how they are afflicted in his affliction.

How true it is that silence is golden, speech is but silver. After a whole week of silent sympathy, which was like balm to the wounded spirit, they venture to speak. Eliphaz the Temanite, perhaps because the eldest, speaks first. In the gentlest and most graceful way he speaks as friend should speak to friend, frankly, candidly and with dignity. He suggests very clearly the belief that Job had brought this great distress upon himself, yet he is very kindly. He refers to this belief as that which all alike held—the orthodox belief of the time, as indeed it was. Then, to soften as much as possible the blow he felt compelled to give, he puts it in the graceful form of a poetic vision, saying,

THE HEROISM OF ENDURANCE. 57

> " Now a thing was secretly brought to me,
> And mine ear received a whisper thereof.
> In thoughts from the visions of the night,
> When deep sleep falleth on men,
> Fear came upon me, and trembling,
> Which made all my bones to shake.
> Then a spirit passed before my face;
> The hair of my flesh stood up:
> It stood still, but I could not discern the appearance thereof:
> A form was before mine eyes:
> There was silence, and I heard a voice saying,
> Shall mortal man be more just than God?
> Shall a man be more pure than his Maker?"

Thus the old gentleman sets forth the universal imperfection of mankind, and paves an easy road for Job to come to confession. Then he frankly urges him to come now and confess his sin to God, and thus seek for mercy and forgiveness:

> " But as for me, I would seek unto God,
> And unto God would I commit my cause;
> Which doeth great things and unsearchable. . . .
> For he maketh sore, and bindeth up;
> He woundeth, and his hands make whole.
> He shall deliver thee in six troubles;
> Yea, in seven there shall no evil touch thee. . . .
> Thou shalt come to thy grave in a full age,
> Like as a shock of corn cometh in in its season.
> Lo this, we have searched it, so it is;
> Hear it, and know thou it for thy good."

An exhortation to repentance could not be more gracefully put, nor more honestly. Job answers it in the same straightforward way. "I know," said he—"I know that it is so: But how can man be just with God?" He does not claim to be without sin, but he does claim to be guiltless of any such sin as they imply in their speech. He claimed to be just what God testified that he was, a complete and honest man, who did his duty as he saw it. He claimed "integrity," which is moral soundness. But his friends will not believe him, and so the discussion goes on, the friends taking their stand on what they regard as an undeniable first principle, namely, that God is a just ruler, and therefore metes out happiness and affliction as the reward of virtue or the penalty of sin. Job does not at first deny this; it is evidently what he too had held, and it involves so much of truth that he is bewildered as to where the fallacy lies. But he has a fact which he will not give up for all the theories he ever held: he is firm in the testimony of a good conscience. On this he stands, as, long after, Martin Luther stood, confident that God would not condemn him when his conscience did not. Now comes what was perhaps the crucial test of his patience. His friends speak in turn, and each presses a little further the accusations of guilt and becomes a little more direct and specific in his charges, till at length they all three lose their temper and become abusive. Eliphaz, who was so dignified and gentle at the first, who clothed his exhortation in the offenceless form of a vision, now becomes almost brutal in his accusations:

"Is not thy wickedness great?
 Neither is there any end to thine iniquities.
 For thou hast taken pledges of thy brother for nought,
 And stripped the naked of their clothing.
 Thou hast not given water to the weary to drink,
 And thou hast withholden bread from the hungry. . . .
 Thou hast sent widows away empty,
 And the arms of the fatherless have been broken."

Bildad and Zophar follow the lead of Eliphaz; they berate Job, call him hard names, abuse him for talking so much and complain that he does not show them proper respect. In short, there is scarcely a mean, unmanly thing in all the catalogue of meanness that they do not accuse him of. So utterly silly and unreasonable do even good men become when they lose their temper. Their elegant language has become common and brutal, their profound philosophy is made absurd by their extremity, and their politeness is torn to rags and tatters; they were "mad." Let this be a warning to us, for just so foolish and undignified do we become when we get angry.

We need not follow into further detail the tedious repetition of their railing, for it is mere railing now. We have seen enough already to convince us that the point is reached, and long past, where you or I should have lost control of tongue and temper and would have answered back in rage. The natural impulse to render railing for railing would lead most men, in such a case, to pour out such floods of boiling words as outraged innocence could find, to hurl hard names and hissing contempt from fiery tongues, to revile the revilers.

But what did Job do?

The answer cannot be given in a word or two, but it is given in the vivid picture which the book presents of noble patience, dignified self-control. It is not that he says anything so brilliant, though his words are often eloquent; it is not that he composes epigrams that may be taken as a motto or illuminated for the decoration of a church. On the contrary, it is ever one of the chief difficulties in the way of patience becoming a popular grace that it offers no opportunity for brilliant achievement. "It vaunteth not itself." When a boiler is carrying enormous pressure of steam there is nothing to indicate it to one who looks on; any unusual appearance in the metal would be a sign of weakness and a cause of alarm. A boiler that explodes is not so good as one that does not, but it attracts a great deal more attention. So it is with the power of endurance in mind and soul as well as in matter: excellence and display do not go together. It is the man who endures most and makes no sign that attains the highest excellence.

But the sublime quality of Job's patience appears in this, that he endured all this not with the dull and stolid temper of one whose sensibilities are blunt; on the contrary, he was a man of most delicate feeling, and almost all circumstances combined to make him keenly sensitive. He had been "the greatest of all the men of the east," and doubtless was accustomed to receive the highest honor and most respectful courtesy from all who approached him; he was not accustomed to being charged with crime or meanness. He was a gentleman, and would keenly feel the rudeness of his friends; from the rabble he could have received it with contempt, but from friends whom he respected it was bitterly unkind.

Such were the tests to which the patience of this

noble man was put. Certainly the vast majority of men would have found their stock of patience utterly exhausted, and would have raved in what they would regard as "righteous indignation." Here and there is found a man who could have bitten his lips and *silently* endured it all. As a beast will shrug himself in the corner of his field and bear the winter's storm, so some men could wrap the cloak of silent dignity about them and with a sort of dogged resignation suffer thus. But this is not the highest kind of patience. Job did not take refuge in silence, but spoke out boldly and freely in self-defence. He does not cease to maintain his integrity; he does not take the air of injured innocence; there are no tears in his voice when he answers the bitter charges of his angry friends. An occasional flash of sarcasm is seen, but even this never exceeds the limits of courteous debate:

> "No doubt but ye are the people,
> And wisdom shall die with you.
> But I have understanding as well as you;
> I am not inferior to you:
> Yea, who knoweth not such things as these?"

These are sharp words, but not with the acid of anger. So all the way through he does not hesitate to strike in self-defence, and good sound ringing blows he gives, but they are arguments, not railing or abuse. Job's patience was not mere non-resistance: it was the much more delicate and difficult task of maintaining the right while suffering wrong. He owed it to the cause of truth as well as of justice to vindicate his character if possible; if not, still to assert the truth and wait for God's good time to bring the evidence. So he fights for his honor as for life; he answers the accusations of his friends with flat denial; he rebukes their conduct, yet says no word unkind or unduly severe. "He was reviled, yet he reviled not again; when he suffered he threatened not, but committed himself to Him that judgeth righteously." Toward God he was humble and submissive; he suffered, but worshiped. Toward the world, which he loved with an honest, open-hearted love, he looked back with regret, but without repining. Toward his friends, in whom he was disappointed, he maintained a dignified defence and a kindly temper. Such was the patience of Job.

I submit to you that there is no more sublime and Christ-like grace, no one in all the catalogue of virtues that demands such high and godlike powers. In patience there is no place for small ambition, which craves the world's applause; no place for the stimulus of passion, which makes even cowards brave on the exciting field of battle. Down in the silent depths of the soul the battle must be fought, the raging passions held with a hand steady enough to give them justice and yet restraint. And when you have succeeded the world will not place the victor's crown upon your brow, for you will have but poorly succeeded if the world knows anything of the battle you have fought. You will, however, have the much more precious rewards, an approving conscience and the favor of your Father in heaven. You will have attained a good degree in the grace which is pre-eminently Christ-like, which the glorious company of the apostles praise and which the noble army of the martyrs exemplify to their unceasing honor.

Patience will never be a popular grace; it costs too much and makes too little show for that. The world likes virtues that glitter more and that go off with a louder report, but Christianity gives the place of honor to that grace which suffers long and still is kind; that does not vaunt itself, is not puffed up; does not behave itself unseemly, seeks not its own, and is not easily provoked; which bears all things, believes all things, hopes all things and endures all things. Such is the greatest of all graces, the grace that never fails. Call it charity or love or patience, or by what name you please, it is and ever will be the high-water mark of Christian attainment. Moreover, it is a most powerful grace; in its influence on the world it is, perhaps, the most efficient of all. Good men are "the light of the world;" their influence is like that of the gentle sunshine, without violence, silently, gently and by gradually increasing power brightening and blessing the world. There is no escape from this kind of influence. When our position is assailed by force of argument we instinctively fortify ourselves against it; just as soon as a man begins to hammer us with logic we harden ourselves and feel that our honor is somehow involved in a successful resistance. But when we see a Christian suffer well, strong in adversity, calm in sorrow, contented in a hard lot, gentle under wrong and patient under outrage and contumely, our admiration is aroused; we feel that there is something great and godlike in this—a reality that logic cannot change, a sweet influence to which honest hearts of every creed give welcome access. There are many things that you can melt but never break.

The kingdom of our Lord Jesus Christ is founded

on forgiveness, and it is distinguished chiefly by the grace of patience.

The "Prince of Peace" is the "Lamb of God." His victories are all the fruit of a most marvelous endurance. The law of his kingdom is, "Do right, endure as a good soldier of Christ, and leave the rest to God." Alas, how often we are careful and troubled about many things, and cumbered with much serving! Let us remember the words,

"They also serve who only stand and wait."

CHAPTER V.

AN ANCIENT CREED.

"I know that my Redeemer liveth."

TRUTH is always true, ever the same. There is a sense, therefore, in which a creed, if true at any time, is true at all times. The principles of morals and religion do not change. God's purposes are absolute. The promise made to our first parents that the seed of the woman should bruise the serpent's head contains the everlasting gospel; it contains the whole of the gospel, as the Child who lay in the manger at Bethlehem was the same as the Man who "suffered under Pontius Pilate, was crucified, dead, and buried." There is but one gospel; it is the "same yesterday, to-day and for ever." But the revelation of this gospel is progressive. In each age "we know in part, and we prophesy in part." Each age, standing on the shoulders of the ages gone, is able to reach higher and see with a wider horizon. We see in Scripture history very many illustrations of the way in which the pinnacles of one man's faith and knowledge become the corner-stones on which the next man builds more stately temples. See, for example, how the Benedictus or Magnificat is built upon the Pentateuch and Psalms. What the flower is to the plant the gospel is to the old dispensation—the same life, the same identity, but with a fuller development and richer beauty.

The history of the Church shows how God has led his people by ways that often seem mysterious and dark. But this is not the wandering of the blind led by the blind; it is not the trying of one way till that failed, and then the trying of another. It is not experiment, but the all-wise providence of Him who knows the end from the beginning and who makes no mistakes. The rainbow in the cloud is the symbol of the everlasting covenant; it is but a single arch; it stretches all the way from the gate of the garden of Eden to the pearly gates of that city whose maker and builder is God. To know God's truth in its fullness we must know it in its order. There is great importance in what Dr. Gibson has so happily termed the "perspective of Scripture history." The relations of time and place, the sequence of events, are often essential to their meaning and always important to their perfect comprehension.

In the book of Job we have a very interesting view of a good man's belief in very early times. It is interesting not only on account of its great antiquity, but especially because of its unique and somewhat remarkable position. It stands, apparently, outside the pale of the Old-Testament Church, and has a certain catholicity about it that is not found in the Mosaic dispensation. We believe "in the Holy Catholic Church," and so did the prophets of the old dispensation, but with a difference. They believed in the future catholicity of the Church, but, for the time then being, the Church was not so, but was exclusive in its very constitution. From the time of Abraham, Israel was a separated people, a nation called and set apart for a special purpose—namely, that through them all nations might be blessed. There was always a door by which a man of any nation might come in and share the covenant blessings of this chosen race, but practically the Church from Abraham to Christ was strictly exclusive, literally the seed of Abraham. But the separation of that people and the giving to them of special privileges did not "disannul the promises," and the promise was a blessing for all nations of the earth. St. Paul claims the blessing promised to Abraham and to his seed as the inheritance of the Christian Church. "If ye be Christ's then are ye Abraham's seed, and heirs according to the promise." St. Peter also, though with difficulty, apprehended the truth, that "in every nation he that feareth God, and worketh righteousness, is accepted with him."

The book of Job, though possibly written by a child of Abraham, does not present Job as a member of that chosen race. Whether we suppose him to have lived before the call of Abraham, or to have lived outside the special covenant, in either case the form of his faith lacks the peculiar features of the Old-Testament symbols and phraseology. His God is not spoken of as the "God of Abraham, Isaac and Jacob;" no covenant is referred to, no temple or tabernacle, no Aaronic priesthood and no Sinaitic ritual. There are the same great truths, as we shall see, but the architecture, so to speak, is different. It is high and catholic, and above all reverent. Let us look at it.

The fundamental article in every creed is that which states what we believe concerning God. The Israelitish creed began with this: "Hear, O Israel; The Lord our God is one Lord."

In our familiar creed we begin with the same

article: "I believe in God the Father Almighty, maker of heaven and earth."

So in the book of Job we find the most prominent article of faith is this belief in God as the Almighty Creator of heaven and earth. Nowhere do we have such a sublime picture of creation as in this book. The very words ring with a poetic grandeur in keeping with the grandeur of the theme:

> "He stretcheth out the north over empty space,
> And hangeth the earth upon nothing. . . .
> He closeth in the face of his throne,
> And spreadeth his cloud upon it. . . .
> The pillars of heaven tremble
> And are astonished at his rebuke. . . .
> By his spirit the heavens are garnished;
> His hand hath pierced the swift serpent.
> Lo, these are but the outskirts of his ways;
> And how small a whisper do we hear of him!
> But the thunder of his power who can understand?"

The closing chapters also, though not the words of Job, may properly be taken as his conception of God's work of creation and providence. In them the writer of the book celebrates the glory of God as revealed in nature. The rolling thunder, the dreadful lightning, the hail, the snow, the furious tempest and the silent frost are cited as the witnesses of power and wisdom in Him who laid earth's corner-stone

> "When the morning stars sang together,
> And all the sons of God shouted for joy."

The great sea, rushing into being, yet shut up with bars and doors, and controlled by the divine command, "Hitherto shalt thou come, but no further; and here shall thy proud waves be stayed,"—all this is pictured with the brief clear strokes of the true poet.

Again and again the phenomena of nature are celebrated in the most appreciative strains. The ordinance of day and night, the time of the dayspring, the preparation of supplies of snow and hail, are each observed. Then, rising with his theme, the poet reviews the sparkling constellations of the bright eastern sky. In the graceful imagery so native to the Oriental mind he presents them in the figures of an ancient mythology. The peculiar antithesis of Hebrew poetry is also used with fine effect: The Pleiades bound like a cluster of diamonds; Orion rejoicing in his freedom; the Mazzaroth (the signs of the Zodiac) led forth like noble steeds upon their course; the Bear and her train wandering in the darkness of the northern sky; and all the ordinances of Heaven ruling in some mysterious way the destinies of men.

Such was Job's conception of the great Creator and Ruler of heaven and earth. But such was by no means the whole nor the highest idea he had of the divine Being.

He does not regard him as merely the powerful and wise Creator of heaven and earth, but also, and much more, as a tender friend. He who by his Spirit hath garnished the heavens does not overlook the humblest of his creatures. He nourisheth the plants with dew and rain, not only in the parks and gardens for the use of man, but

> "In the lonely valley
> And on the mountains high,
> And in the silent wilderness,
> Where no man passeth by."

He who fastened the gates of the shadow of death does not fail to feed the young ravens when they cry, and he satisfies the hungry appetite of the young lions. The working of God's providence, his care for all creatures, is a theme of which Job never seems to weary; again and again, even in the depths of his distress, he breaks forth in most enthusiastic song of the wonderful works of God.

We hear much now-a-days of conflict between science and religion, as though the Bible was somehow out of sympathy with nature; but such a thought could rise only in minds densely ignorant of the most important books of holy Scripture. Read the book of Job, and tell me where you can find in all the sneering pages ever penned by infidelity such intense and intelligent appreciation of nature as is here. It is broad, and in this it differs greatly from the narrow, theory-bound admiration of so many small scientists and petty theologians. It is poetical, yet free from the sickly sentimentalism that is too often the blemish of religio-scientific discussion. There is no attempt to exalt nature into a god and the love of the beautiful into a cult, neither is there any suggestion that "the trail of the serpent is over them all." There is no cynicism in the whole book. Even in the saddest hours of his affliction Job does not descend to the folly of railing against the course of nature. He cries out in his agony for death to come to his relief; he saw then as he had never seen before the insecurity of earthly hopes and the certainty of trouble. He felt then as he had never felt before the insignificance of man in the great world which he inhabits only as a pilgrim and a sojourner for a night. Yet in all this there is no fault-finding, but an honest love for the good and beautiful things of earth.

He believed in God the Father Almighty, maker of heaven and earth; and he believed in creation as the work of God. It would be well for us if we would add this last clause to our creed also.

But this ancient creed was not merely speculative; it was eminently practical. In all this reference to God's power and wisdom there is a practical lesson inferred. It was by the study of God's work of creation and providence that Job's own hope was confirmed and his confidence maintained. The thought which runs through all is that He who gives such evidence of power, wisdom and love for all cannot do wrong. "Shall not the judge of all the earth do right?"

The only hope and consolation that endured through all the dark and dismal day was this: God rules above the storm; "Underneath are the everlasting arms." The rock which saved Job's faith was this convincing evidence that in this universe there is a God whose wisdom none can doubt and whose power and care for all is manifest. The greatness of Job appears in this, that even when he found his former theory of providence to be wrong he does not give up all for lost, but, avoiding despair on the one hand and cutting loose from his false philosophy on the other, he swings clear of everything that can by any means be shaken, and with serenest confidence holds fast to the simple, childlike creed,

> "Behold, the fear of the Lord, that is wisdom;
> And to depart from evil is understanding."

He had the courage to "do right whatever comes of it." His prayer is ever for God's guidance in a world too great for him to comprehend:

> "Lead, kindly light, amid the encircling gloom,
> Lead thou me on;
> The night is dark and I am far from home;
> Lead thou me on.
> Keep thou my feet; I do not ask to see
> The distant scene; one step enough for me."

But while Job believed thus firmly in the providence of God, believed that this world was under fixed and prudent laws, by which all creatures are assigned their places and given a destiny suited to their capacity, he believed that far above all this God was a friend of those who do his will. God's love for Job is vastly more than providential care for a creature; it is a personal love; it is friendship. God does not say to Satan, "Hast thou considered the scheme of nature upon the earth, what a perfect system it is? Hast thou observed the order of creation, and the evolution age by age of higher and nobler forms of life?" By no means; though these things are doubtless well worth considering, the thought here is much higher and better. "Hast thou considered my servant Job? a perfect and an upright man." Why, he knows his servant by name; knows his character and circumstances; knows him as friend knows friend, and speaks of him with admiration and respect! Ah, yes; man is a small weak creature in this universe, but the man who has Jehovah's friendship, the man of whom Almighty God speaks with interest and respect, has a crown of glory that outshines all the stars of heaven. What dignity it gives to every life to know that God takes pleasure in it and that all its works are ordained of him!

Our Christian creeds, as a rule, pass on directly from the being, attributes and work of God to the special acts of providence for our redemption. The incarnation and earthly life and passion of our Saviour are unquestionably the most important facts accomplished since the world was made, and may very properly be considered in this order; but the order of events is usually the reverse of the order of plan or purpose. If, for example, I wish to reach the top of the stairway, I can do so only from the step next to the top, and I can reach that one only from the next below; this is the order of my plan; it begins with the point to be reached—the object—and selects means for reaching that object. In the execution of the plan the order is reversed: I must start from where I am, and end with that which was first in thought—the object.

All the means to our salvation were included in God's purpose from the beginning; the incarnation, the passion and the resurrection were present realities in the divine mind. But they became accomplished facts only in the fullness of time. Job lived long before the incarnation; whatever he knew of the plan of redemption he knew as God's promise, not as history. It may be instructive to observe what conception of salvation Job was able to form.

We gather from his words the following points:

He believed, first, in the absolute sovereignty of God;

Second, that all men are guilty before God;

Third, that God by his free grace saves those who call upon him.

This seems, perhaps, a meagre creed, but it is a very comprehensive one. An outline map may be just as perfect in its way as one that gives all the details. The simple rules of addition and division are just as necessary to the great mathematician as to the child who knows nothing beyond them. So this creed of Job concerning the purpose of redemption is as accurate as could be framed to-day, though not so full.

These are, after all, the great essential truths,—God's sovereignty, man's guilt and salvation by free grace. It is the strength of our faith, the loyalty of our adherence to the great essentials, rather than our knowledge of the details of doctrine that determines our character. All truth is precious, and willingness to accept truth as we find it is a grace to be sought for by every one with prayer and fasting. But the notion that God limits his gift of salvation to the sect or party that is able to frame the most accurate statement of doctrine is so wretchedly absurd that the virtual teaching of it by not a few is a matter of amazement and shame.

One more article of Job's creed is worthy of

notice, namely, his belief in the resurrection. The familiar text, "I know that my Redeemer liveth, and that he shall stand at the latter day upon the earth: and though after my skin worms destroy this body, yet in my flesh shall I see God: whom I shall see for myself, and mine eyes shall behold, and not another; though my reins be consumed within me,"—this text has been the subject of much controversy. As it stands in the common version, it teaches the doctrine of the resurrection very clearly. But the belief that Job intended to teach this has probably led the translator to give a very liberal rendering of the passage; at all events, it is a very liberal rendering, and can scarcely be regarded as more than a fair paraphrase of the thought.

Yet after all this is admitted it remains true that this traditional rendering of the passage is essentially correct. Job did look for a redeemer, a vindicator, who should appear after his decease. He had given up the hope he had cherished so long that God would restore him, and thus vindicate his character; he feels that he shall die under the cloud of the world's condemnation. He has surrendered without conditions, and sighs, with weary heart,

> "Know now that God hath overthrown me. ....
> He hath fenced up my way that I cannot pass. ....
> He hath destroyed me on every side, and I am gone:
> And mine hope hath he removed like a tree."

He has reached the lowest point of his humiliation. He cries out for pity. His servants desert him, his friends revile him, and the very children on the street mock him. Does he despair? Does this sound like despair?

> "Oh that my words were now written!
> Oh that they were inscribed in a book!
> That with an iron pen and lead
> They were graven in the rock for ever!
> But I know that my redeemer liveth,
> And that he shall stand up at the last upon the earth:
> And after my skin hath been thus destroyed,
> Yet from my flesh shall I see God:
> Whom I shall see for myself,
> And mine eyes shall behold, and not another."

He has lost all hope of earth, but he is rich in hope in God. He has loosed his grasp of this world, but only to tighten his grip upon the Rock of ages. He has loved this world with an honest, manly love, but when God takes it from him he is able to say, "He gave; he takes; blessed be his name." Buffeted by Satan, afflicted, tormented and brought down to the dust of humiliation, to the shadow of death, we look in pity, and wait with tearful sympathy to hear his dying groans; but it is the shout of a conqueror that breaks upon our ear. It is but another wording of the grand triumphal song,

"Death is swallowed up in victory.
O death, where is thy sting?
O grave, where is thy victory?
Thanks be to God, which giveth us the victory."

CHAPTER VI.

MYSTERIOUS PROVIDENCE.

WE read that "the way of transgressors is hard," and our instinct of justice responds, "It ought to be." The fitness of things seems to require that integrity and prosperity should go hand-in-hand. It is assumed that perfect government will secure the welfare of the good and the overthrow of the wicked. Our faith relies on the promise, "He that walketh uprightly walketh surely," and the common-sense of men expects the same. In almost every language there are proverbs that assert or imply that "godliness is profitable unto all things, having promise of the life that now is and of that which is to come."

The substantial truth of this belief is hardly open to doubt, yet as a theory of life by which to explain the works of providence it has never been quite satisfactory. Thoughtful men in every age have noticed with surprise and disappointment that "there be just men to whom it happeneth according to the work of the wicked, and there be wicked men to whom it happeneth according to the work of the righteous."

Not only does all nature seem quite blind to moral worth, and "red in tooth and claw," but the whole order of providential government fails to show, in mortal sight, that favor toward the good which we are apt to look for. Like the Psalmist, we are often "vexed" to see how prosperous the wicked are, while men "of whom the world is not worthy" are "destitute, afflicted, tormented."

How is this, and why is it? is the question which the larger part of the book of Job discusses.

The question is not stated in the abstract, but in a concrete case—Job's case; nor is the author's aim quite as ambitious as that of the great poet who wrote the greatest English epic to

"assert eternal providence,
And justify the ways of God to man."

The purpose of the book of Job (it is well to recognize it from the first) is neither to explain nor to "justify" the ways of God to men, but rather to show that they are beyond our comprehension, that it is impossible that they should be, in all cases, made plain to mortal man. And the most prominent lesson of the book is that our inability to justify his ways gives no ground at all for doubting that they are both just and kind. On the contrary, a providence that we could always understand would be a very poor and petty providence.

The case under discussion is briefly this: Job, a perfect and an upright man, is introduced to us in the height of prosperity. Health and wealth, honor and a happy household, fill his cup. He is at once a God-fearing man and "the greatest of the men of the East." It is not asserted that his prosperity was due to his piety, but the two are so associated as to imply more than accidental connection. Suddenly, and with no reason that any mortal man could see, a series of most frightful calamities befall him. These misfortunes are not due to any one cause, but to various forces over which Job has no control, therefore implying no fault on his part, nor any lack of wisdom. They were clearly providential, *i. e.* due to causes which could not be foreseen or controlled. They were what the law still calls "the act of God."

These were all the facts in the case as it could be known to Job and his friends. The question is, How can such facts be reconciled with our faith in a righteous providence governing all creatures and all their actions?

There are some answers which the author of this book did not think worth noticing. There is the atheist's answer, "There is no God, and therefore no providence. Job had bad luck, and that is the whole of it."

The agnostic answers, "Job lost his oxen and asses by robbery perpetrated by some party or parties unknown, supposed to have been Sabeans. The sheep were killed by lightning; the Chaldeans 'lifted' the cattle; a cyclone caused the death of his children; while Job's disease was evidently brought on by natural causes that had nothing remarkable about them. As for any overruling providence, it is an utterly unscientific hypothesis," etc.

Others would answer that it was the work of some evil spirit, or of those principles of evil which war against the good.

The latter two of these answers have a certain amount of truth in them. Both natural causes and the evil spirit are distinctly recognized, and their place in the chain of causation plainly mentioned. The error of the agnostic is in supposing that by thus reciting the instrumental causes he has in any degree approached the solution of the real problem or exhausted the field of profitable thought concerning man's relation to God. To thoughtful men there is something repulsive in such flippant treatment of questions that have such intimate relation to the highest and most practical duties of life. Much the same thing may be said of those who rest the subject on the supposition that it was the work of evil spirits. That is true, but is not sufficient. The only question worth discussing lies back of all this.

The friends of Job were bigoted, perhaps, but they were too broad-minded, too thoughtful, to imagine that this was a question to be settled by any mere inspection of the instruments employed. All parties in the book agree that these afflictions came by the permission of a sovereign God. There is no quibbling over mere terms, no talk of fate or natural law or principle of evil warring against the principle of good. They proceed directly to the great question, Why has God done thus? They vie with one another in their confession of faith in God's sovereign providence. Job is the first to speak. "Then Job arose, and rent his mantle, and shaved his head, and fell down upon the ground, and worshiped; and he said, Naked came

I out of my mother's womb, and naked shall I return thither: the Lord gave, and the Lord hath taken away; blessed be the name of the Lord."

Eliphaz clothes his confession in poetic imagery, a vision, and a voice saying, "Shall mortal man be more just than God? shall man be more pure than his Maker?"

Bildad puts his creed more bluntly: "Doth God pervert judgment? or doth the Almighty pervert justice?"

Zophar continues in the same high tone:

"Canst thou by searching find out God?
Canst thou find out the Almighty unto perfection?
It is high as heaven: what canst thou do?
Deeper than Sheol: what canst thou know?"

They agree in these two points: God is sovereign, and God is just; absolutely sovereign, and infinitely just. But from this point their creeds diverge. In answer to the question how God can be just and yet afflict the righteous, the three friends stoutly deny that he ever does afflict them. They are unanimous in their belief that uprightness secures prosperity. To deny this is, in their minds, infidelity. If the wicked prospers at all, it is only for a little while, and in order that his destruction may be the more terrible when it comes. Reduced to its simplest terms, their theory was simply *quid pro quo*—so much righteousness for so much prosperity.

According to this rule they judge Job's case and account for his misfortunes. They tell him, kindly and with evident sympathy, but none the less positively, that he is suffering the righteous penalty of great wickedness. They do not deny that he had given every evidence of being a good man, but they know, as we do, that appearances are no certain index of the heart's condition. They did not consider the good repute of Job sufficient reason for setting aside what they regarded as a well-established doctrine of divine justice, and they were quite right in their ruling on the point. The odor of sanctity may create a presumption of innocence, but it cannot be pleaded in answer to facts or well-established principles. In this case the facts were not accessible; they must decide on general principles. According to these, Job's affliction proved his wickedness.

Against this Job has nothing to answer, except the assertion of his own innocence. He can only plead "Not guilty," and appeal to his good standing in the community to give some value to his assertion. This was his whole case, and it was still further weakened by the fact that he could not claim absolute innocence; he was only relatively pure, guiltless of such uncommon sin as his unusual misfortunes indicated, on their theory.

The friends, very naturally, refuse to see in this answer any good ground for setting aside a well-established theory of providence. The case was closed; it could not be argued any farther on this line.

But these friends are not a court to whose decision Job felt bound to submit; they are simply friends who have volunteered to give advice, and who become offended, as such friends so often do, because their advice is not accepted. Their advice was kindly given, but it involved the assumption of Job's great guilt and hypocrisy. This he will not admit, and therefore he appeals from their judgment by calling in question their whole theory of providence. He boldly raises the question, Does God always reward the righteous and afflict the wicked? He does not quite deny this, but he calls it in question. He cites some facts hard to account for on the supposition that it is so. He throws the burden of proof on those who have asserted it to convict him, and thus it becomes the burning question of the book. Each friend in turn brings this doctrine of divine rewards and punishments in this world and fairly hurls it at Job's head. Eliphaz first puts it thus:

"Remember, I pray thee, who ever perished, being innocent?
 Or where were the righteous cut off?
 Even as I have seen, they that plough iniquity, and sow wickedness, reap the same.
 By the blast of God they perish, and by the breath of his nostrils are they consumed."

Bildad follows in the same strain:

"If thou wert pure and upright; surely now he would awake for thee, and make the habitation of thy righteousness prosperous. . . .
 Can the rush grow up without mire? can the flag grow without water?
 Whilst it is yet in his greenness, and not cut down, it withereth before any other herb.
 So are the paths of all that forget God; and the hypocrite's hope shall perish. . . .
 He shall lean upon his house, but it shall not stand: he shall hold it fast, but it shall not endure. . . .
 Behold, God will not cast away a perfect man, neither will he help the evil-doers."

Zophar, more briefly, but to the same effect:

"The eyes of the wicked shall fail, and they shall not escape, and their hope shall be as the giving up of the ghost."

Job, thus goaded, breaks out with a bold denial of the facts, and asserts that just the opposite is true:

> "No doubt but ye are the people, and wisdom shall die with you.
> But I have understanding as well as you; I am not inferior to you: yea, who knoweth not such things as these?
> I am as one mocked of his neighbor, who calleth upon God, and he answereth him: the just, upright man is laughed to scorn.
> He that is ready to slip with his feet is as a lamp despised in the thought of him that is at ease.
> The tabernacles of robbers prosper, and they that provoke God are secure: into whose hand God bringeth abundantly."

Job is thoroughly aroused, perhaps a little excited. He is apparently alarmed at his own boldness. It seems even to him very little short of blasphemy to deny that God deals out prosperity like rations to the children of men, according to their deserts. But he is convinced that there is something radically wrong with a theory that has to ignore so many facts. He has begun to cite these facts, and plunges ahead to the very border of impious challenge of God's justice:

> "He leadeth counsellors away spoiled, and maketh the judges fools.
> He looseth the bond of kings, and girdeth their loins with a girdle.

> He leadeth princes away spoiled, and overthroweth the mighty. . . .
> He poureth contempt upon princes, and weakeneth the strength of the mighty. . . .
> He taketh away the heart of the chief of the people of the earth, and causeth them to wander in a wilderness where there is no way."

The utter pettiness of their theory becomes more apparent to him as he reviews the facts of history. Yet he speaks as one who feels the fainting sensation of collapsing orthodoxy. He has broken with the old doctrine, and is at sea, sure only of this, that whatever truth was, it was not their doctrine. "Horror took hold of him," he says, when he first faced the fact that the wicked often prosper, while the godly are afflicted and apparently forsaken. It seemed to imply utter carelessness, if not injustice, on the part of God's all-ruling providence. Nevertheless, the fact remains,

> "Wherefore do the wicked live, become old, yea, are mighty in power?
> Their seed is established in their sight with them and their offspring before their eyes.
> Their houses are safe from fear, neither is the rod of God upon them."

He anticipates the answer, that they are reserved for the day of destruction, they shall be brought forth in the day of wrath. He replies by denying the fact. The wicked often die without dishonor:

"One dieth in his full strength, being wholly at ease and quiet. . . . The clods of the valley shall be sweet unto him, and every man shall draw after him. . . . How then comfort ye me in vain, seeing in your answers there remaineth falsehood?"

How often it is so even now! The godly, generous, kindly man lives a life of toil and sorrow and misfortune, while the selfish worldling prospers by hardness and sharp-dealing. It is certain that if success is what we are apt to regard it—namely, the acquisition of the good things of this world—then honesty is not always good policy, nor is godliness profitable. What then? Is there no such thing as providence? or does providence ignore all moral considerations, and govern the world according to blind natural law? Job is not willing to go so far as either of these suppositions, and it is greatly to the credit of his self-control that he is not. A mind less delicately poised than was his would almost certainly have fallen into some such error as this in its reaction from the theory that was used to convict him, and which he sees to be inadequate to the facts. But Job is never small;

he is weary sometimes, but never weak; extreme sometimes, but never absurd. His doubt and dismay in view of what he sees to be a problem too great for any easy solution makes him all the more impatient with the tedious homilies of his friends in defence of their neat but petty doctrines. He confesses that he cannot account for the facts himself, but he argues that that is no reason for accepting a false explanation. Better leave the whole question unsolved than to attempt to justify the ways of God to man by falsehood.

"Will ye speak wickedly for God? and talk deceitfully for him?" There is very delicate sarcasm in this question. To put it more coarsely, it amounts to saying, "Is God such a client that you, as his advocate, must resort to a defence which you know is not sincere? It is surely wiser in such a case to confess your ignorance."

"Oh that ye would altogether hold your peace! and it should be your wisdom."

This is virtually the end of the debate. The friends reiterate their views and intensify their accusations, trying, as we so often do, to make emphatic repetition do the work of sound reasoning and abusive language take the place of facts, but there is nothing new advanced in support of either side. They all seem to feel, though the friends will not confess it, that the problem of God's providence is vaster and more difficult of solution than they had ever imagined it before. Eliphaz answers again at considerable length, Bildad very briefly, and Zophar not at all. Then Job closes the discussion with a long review. He goes over the whole case, looking carefully on all sides of it. He is like a prisoner looking for some way of escape. His confidence in God's justice is absolute, but how this terrible affliction which he is suffering is consistent with that justice he cannot understand. He seems almost to forget the presence of his friends and to be entirely absorbed in his efforts to find God. This review of the case which we have in chapters 26–31 is in many respects the most beautiful section of the book.

He first reviews the evidence of God's omnipotent sovereignty. He looks out upon the world, and in sublimest poetry magnifies the power and wisdom of God:

"Sheol is naked before him,
And Abaddon hath no covering.
He stretcheth out the north over empty space,
And hangeth the earth upon nothing. . . .
He closeth in the face of his throne,

> And spreadeth his cloud upon it. . . .
> By his spirit the heavens are garnished;
> And his hand hath pierced the swift serpent.
> Lo, these are but the outskirts of his ways:
> And how small a whisper do we hear of him!
> The thunder of his power who can understand?"

Then he turns again to his own experience, as if to see whether what he has just said of God's power and wisdom will enable him to understand his own case. He repeats with a solemn oath the protest of his innocence:

> "Till I die I will not put away mine integrity from me.
> My righteousness I hold fast, and will not let it go;
> My heart doth not reproach me for any of my days."

Then he turns to his accusers with a most surprising picture of the hopelessness of the godless and their certain destruction and disgrace:

> "For what is the hope of the godless, though he get him gain,
> When God taketh away his soul? . . .
> For God shall hurl at him, and not spare:
> He would fain flee out of his hand.
> Men shall clap their hands at him,
> And shall hiss him out of his place."

It is very surprising to hear this from Job, for it is just what he has seemed to deny heretofore. The explanation seems to be that Job is perplexed. He does not deny and never had denied that "the face of the Lord is against them that do evil," but he had denied that there was any such regularity in the dealing of God with men as warranted the conclusion which his friends had drawn from his affliction. He seems to say, "Now here are the facts: God is infinitely wise, and absolutely sovereign. He destroyeth the godless, even as you say. But I am destroyed, being innocent, and on this one fact your whole theory breaks down, and miserable comforters are ye all." He has no doctrine of his own to offer. No modern agnostic has felt more deeply nor expressed so well the utter inability of man to comprehend his own life or to expound the ways of God to man. But this limitation of human understanding, which the agnostic makes the excuse for his denial of the possibility of spiritual wisdom, Job makes the starting-point of a new departure in the search for truth and duty. He is convinced that he cannot comprehend God's providence. What then? Shall he deny the possibility of wisdom too great to be grasped by human intelligence? No; Job reasons better than this. He says the wisdom of God is too vast for him; even in the works of nature about him he sees manifested such wonderful wisdom as he can but feebly admire, how much less criticise. He lets the hand of reason fall, and reaches up the hand of faith. He ceases to ask for reasons, and begins to ask for duty. He has reached the point of preferring a command to an explanation. This is the highest kind of wisdom, and yet it is just this that is most scoffed at by ignorant unbelief. Ignorance that is so dense as to imagine that it knows everything is most hopeless. Ignorance that will not be directed is deepest folly. What then shall we call those who demand that the divine plans and purposes shall submit to the test of human judgment? Can you get a quart of water into a pint cup? Can the whole great ocean give the cup more than it can hold? It is not a question of giving, but of receiving. So is the revelation of God to man limited not by his resources, but by our capacity.

Job sought long and honestly for the reason of God's strange treatment of him. He wanted to know, and why should he not ask and seek and ponder? But when he cannot find what he sought, he takes what he can find. Like the blind man whom Jesus healed on the Sabbath day, when the Jews told him that Jesus was a sinner, he answered, "Whether he be a sinner, I know not: one thing I know, that, whereas I was blind, now I see." So

Job, failing to find an answer to all his questions, falls back on the faith which never wavered. He found rest in the blessed assurance that He who rules in earth as well as heaven knows the end from the beginning and makes no mistakes. Man, therefore, cannot go wrong if he will simply obey. This is the conclusion to which the careful review of the whole subject brought him. It is henceforth the corner-stone of his faith. His doctrine of providence is not so complete, perhaps, as the neat and pretty theory of the three friends, but his doctrine of personal duty is clear as crystal:

> "Behold, the fear of the Lord, that is wisdom;
> And to depart from evil is understanding."

This simple faith is the pure gold that came out of the fire of his affliction, and the poetic confession of it is not surpassed in all the literature of the world. The inspired words are better than any comment.

> "Surely there is a mine for silver,
> And a place for gold which they refine.
> Iron is taken out of the earth,
> And brass is molten out of the stone.
> Man setteth an end to darkness,
> And searcheth out to the furthest bound
> The stones of darkness and of the shadow of death.

He breaketh open a shaft away from where men sojourn;
They are forgotten of the foot that passeth by;
They hang afar from men, they swing to and fro.
As for the earth, out of it cometh bread:
And underneath it is turned up as it were by fire.
The stones thereof are the place of sapphires,
And it hath dust of gold. . . .
He putteth forth his hand upon the flinty rock;
He overturneth the mountains by the roots.
He cutteth out channels among the rocks;
And his eye seeth every precious thing.
He bindeth the streams that they trickle not;
And the thing that is hid bringeth he forth to light.
But where shall wisdom be found?
And where is the place of understanding?
Man knoweth not the price thereof:
Neither is it found in the land of the living.
The deep saith, It is not in me:
The sea saith, It is not with me.
It cannot be gotten for gold,
Neither shall silver be weighed for the price thereof.
It cannot be valued with the gold of Ophir,
With the precious onyx, or the sapphire.
Gold and glass cannot equal it:
Neither shall the exchange thereof be jewels of fine gold.
No mention shall be made of coral or of crystal:
Yea, the price of wisdom is above rubies.
The topaz of Ethiopia shall not equal it,
Neither shall it be valued with pure gold.
Whence then cometh wisdom?
And where is the place of understanding?

> Seeing it is hid from the eyes of all living,
> And kept close from the fowls of the air.
> Destruction and Death say,
> We have heard a rumor thereof with our ears.
> God understandeth the way thereof,
> And he knoweth the place thereof.
> For he looketh to the ends of the earth,
> And seeth under the whole heaven;
> To make a weight for the wind;
> Yea, he meteth out the waters by measure.
> When he made a decree for the rain,
> And a way for the lightning of the thunder:
> Then did he see it and declare it;
> He established it, yea, and searched it out.
> And unto man he said,
> Behold, the fear of the Lord, that is wisdom;
> And to depart from evil is understanding."

We cannot understand our relation to this universe in which we find ourselves. Some one has said, " We are born as on a step of a great stairway; there are steps below us, we know not how many; there are steps above us, leading we know not whither." But we have the blessed assurance that He who sent us hither has a place for us to fill, a destiny for us to reach. In God's great plan our life has a meaning and a purpose which it shall be our glory to accomplish. No life is insignificant that is constantly present to the mind of God. What dignity it adds to the life we now live to know that God " hath ordained the works that we should walk in them " ! Go, therefore, to thy work or warfare with undaunted soul.

" Poor vaunt of life indeed,
  Were man but formed to feed
  On joy, to solely seek and feast.
      Such feasting ended, then
        As sure an end to men;
  Irks care the crop-full bird? Frets doubt the maw-crammed beast?

" Then welcome each rebuff
  That turns earth's smoothness rough,
  Each sting that bids nor sit nor stand, but go.
      Be our joys three parts pain,
        Strive, and hold cheap the strain;
  Learn, nor account the pang; dare, never grudge the throe!

" For thence—a paradox
  Which comforts while it mocks—
  Shall life succeed in that it seems to fail:
      What I aspired to be,
        And was not, comforts me:
  A brute I might have been, but would not sink i' the scale."

CHAPTER VII.

THE YOUNG MAN'S VIEW.

"Lo, all these things doth God work
Twice, yea, thrice, with a man,
To bring back his soul from the pit."

ELIHU is a great puzzle to the critics of the book of Job. His introduction at the very crisis of the narrative, with a long and somewhat tedious discussion of the questions so fully treated already, is against all their notions of what the author ought to have done.

It must be confessed that Elihu does seem to intrude at a moment when we should have least expected him. When we read that "the words of Job are ended," we naturally expect to hear immediately, if ever, that "the Lord answered Job," and in that answer to find the conclusion of the whole matter. We are in an attitude of expectancy. We feel that neither Job nor the three friends have said the last word in the matter. We may be ready to admit that the questions of God's relation to the world and the connection between godliness and prosperity are not so simple and clear as we had imagined; but still to leave the whole field to the agnostic, to imply that these questions are utterly beyond all profitable discussion, seems a lame and impotent conclusion. Moreover, we have heard an appeal taken from the judgment of man to the judgment of God, and we await his answer with great interest. Indeed, there is somewhat more than an appeal to the supreme court of Heaven against the judgment of man. That court has virtually been impeached. It has been hinted that divine justice is, like human justice, blind. Questions have been raised which involve the righteousness of Providence, and the Almighty has been challenged to answer in his own defence. The appeal is audacious, and the interest at this point grows intense.

We are therefore surprised, and perhaps annoyed, to hear not the voice of the Lord, but the voice of a man break the silence. A young man too, not mentioned before, not a party of either part, a mere bystander, cries, "Hearken unto me; I also will show my opinion." If ever a young man took the floor at a disadvantage, Elihu does so. Our sense of propriety is offended, and we are ready to find fault on slight occasion.

He is introduced by the author, and then he proceeds to introduce himself with graceful though rather profuse apologies. Then, with a good deal of assurance for so young and modest a man, he reopens the whole case, threshes a good deal of the old straw over again, and when done leaves us somewhat in doubt as to just wherein he differs from those who have spoken before.

Now, the critics ask, "Why is he introduced at all? Why is he not mentioned in the prologue? Why is he ignored in the conclusion? What is the author's attitude toward Elihu's view of the matter?" These and many other questions have been endlessly discussed, but never answered. Let us leave them to the learned critics, and pass on to hear what the young man has to say.

The author has introduced him briefly as "Elihu, the son of Barachel the Buzite, of the kindred of Ram." But neither the name nor the genealogy gives any clue to the questions just asked concerning him. The only fact made prominent in his introduction is his youth. The author mentions it, Elihu refers to it repeatedly, and his whole manner proclaims it. His impatience with the three friends because they have not been able to answer Job, his confidence of his own ability to answer him, the impetuous rush of his speech, the lack of that stately dignity which so prominently marked the earlier speeches of the others and the frequent use of new words and phrases, —all seem to mark him as belonging to a later generation and a somewhat different school from all the others. Now, it seems probable that these marks of youth are intentionally used by the author to depict a suitable spokesman for a view of Job's case, and of providence in general, which was regarded by the author as new and to some degree in advance of the traditional views set forth by the other speakers. Their view was, as we have seen, that providence is practically a system of rewards and punishments. The righteous prosper, and the wicked are destroyed. This is the law. If any case seems unaccountable, it is only apparently so, for any real exception to this law would imply unrighteousness in God.

Job discards this doctrine of providence, on the ground that it does not accord with all the facts. The wicked, he says, are very often as prosperous as the godly; even more so. And, admitting that the scheme of providence under which we live is such as to favor the good and thwart the wicked, it is only so in a general way, and by no means so absolute a law as to be made the basis of any such conclusions as they had drawn from it.

He further maintained that the scope of providence is so wide, so far beyond our limited horizon, that it is not possible for us to have any knowledge of the whole that could warrant our interpretation of any part. His conclusion is that to us providence is inscrutable, a mystery too deep for human intelligence to fathom. Man must fall back upon the fundamental truths of God's wisdom and power. For man, obedience is wisdom.

"Behold, the fear of the Lord, that is wisdom;
And to depart from evil is understanding."

This was Job's doctrine of providence, and a very good doctrine it is. But in his stout defence of his own integrity he fell into expressions that seem to call in question the absolute justice of God in afflicting him. He sometimes seems to say very plainly, "God has afflicted me without cause."

This is the point at which Elihu attacks him: "His wrath was kindled against Job because he justified himself rather than God." But his wrath was against the three friends also, "because they found no answer, and yet had condemned Job."

The young man is the champion of neither party.

He does not share the view of the friends, that the affliction of Job is proof of his great wickedness. But, on the other hand, he is scarcely less severe in his censure of Job for what he calls his "rebellion." He is shocked at his arrogance in challenging the righteousness of God.

"For Job hath said, I am righteous,
And God hath taken away my right:
Notwithstanding my right I am accounted a liar;
My wound is incurable, though I am without transgression."

What irreverence this is! Elihu exclaims. Was there ever such arrogance heard before!

"What man is like Job,
Who drinketh up scorning like water? . . .
He addeth rebellion unto his sin,
He clappeth his hands among us."

This was Elihu's first "point," and it established his right to speak. He has something to say that has not been said, and which is important. He has put his finger on the one unsound spot in Job's religious system. He does not accuse Job of having done anything to bring this affliction on himself. He does not assume that his affliction is punishment at all, and he censures Job severely for assuming that God is less kind in sending trials than in sending pleasures.

We feel that Elihu is too severe in his censure, that he over-states his case in order to make it clear that he has a case; but in the main he is certainly right. It is perhaps significant that Job does not answer Elihu; he does not deny this charge. Moreover, the Lord seems to imply the same fault when he asks (chap. 40 : 8), "Wilt thou condemn me that thou mayest be justified?" Let us examine this charge, therefore, and see just what is the fault in Job—the only fault the Lord lays to his charge.

Job had said that man's duty is obedience, his highest wisdom is submission to God. In this he is clearly right. But there is a vast difference between the obedience of the slave, who must, and the obedience of the child, who loves and trusts the father who commands. There is a difference also between the complaining obedience of mere consent and the cheerful obedience of enthusiastic service. Now, Job's obedience was somewhat of the former kind. He submits, but he seems to think that the Lord is somewhat under obligation to him for his submission. When his wife lost faith and advised him to renounce God, he answered with indignation,

> "What? shall we receive good at the hand of God,
> And shall we not receive evil?
> In all this did not Job sin with his lips."

Still, there was no trace of the thought that this was *not evil, but good*. His attitude of mind has a strong suggestion of forgiving God for doing him an injury. The thought of affliction being a blessing had never occurred to him or to his friends. This is the thought which the young man Elihu brings forward. The author puts it in the mouth of the young man because it was in his time a novelty. It is so familiar to us that we rarely think of its recent origin, but it was not a familiar doctrine in the Old Testament. It is true we have many texts in the Old Testament that teach the value of affliction, such as "Behold, happy is the man whom God correcteth;" "Therefore despise not thou the chastening of the Almighty;" and "Blessed is the man whom thou chastenest, O Lord, and teachest out of thy law," and many others. But in all these the idea is that it is well for a man to be punished, that he may learn to do right. It is correction that is commended. But the thought which Elihu brings out is different from this. He suggests that the Lord may, and often does, send affliction to men not for what they have done—not as punishment, but as discipline,— whereby they are taught through their own experience wisdom that cannot be otherwise acquired, and developed in beautiful graces which only adversity and sorrow can bring out. Job even at his best seems to have imagined the Lord as keeping a book-account with him, and owing him favors so long as he was loyal and obedient. Elihu does not deny that there is something like this in God's relation to us, but it is an inadequate conception of the matter. Providence in his view is not so much governmental as educational. God's treatment of us is to be judged by the future as well as by the past; by what he has for us to do and to be as well as by what we have done and been.

It is difficult to follow what he says without reading into his words more than he certainly teaches. He was still far from grasping this doctrine in the fullness of its New-Testament statement, "It is for chastening (education) that ye endure: God dealeth with you as with sons: for what son is there whom his father chasteneth (educateth) not?" Nowhere in the Old Testament is this doctrine taught so plainly as it is in the New; but Elihu certainly had the essential thought of it all when he describes how God deals with a man to withdraw him from his purpose:

> "For God speaketh once,
> Yea twice, yet man perceiveth it not.
> In a dream, in a vision of the night,
> When deep sleep falleth upon men,
> In slumberings upon the bed;
> Then he openeth the ears of men,
> And sealeth their instruction,
> That he may withdraw man from his purpose,
> And hide pride from man."

Not only in this way but by other means God strives with men for their good, and seeks to turn them away from doing evil which would destroy them. He even spares their lives that they may learn wisdom and repentance:

> "He keepeth back his soul from the pit,
> And his life from perishing by the sword.
> He is chastened also with pain upon his bed,
> And the multitude of his bones with strong pain. . . .
> Lo, all these things worketh God
> Oftentimes with man,
> To bring back his soul from the pit,
> To be enlightened with the light of the living."

Such is the young man's view of God's dealing with men. This, he seems to say, is the principle by which all God's works of providence must be studied.

Elihu now proceeds to discuss Job's case in the light of this principle. First, he points out the utter absurdity of Job's complaint:

> "For he hath said, It profiteth a man nothing
> That he should delight himself with God. . . .
> Thinkest thou this to be thy right,
> Or sayest thou, My righteousness is more than God's,
> That thou sayest, What advantage will it be unto thee?
> And, What profit shall I have, more than if I had sinned?"

Elihu asks, What does God owe you? You complain of lack of profit: how much then is God in debt to you?

> "If thou be righteous, what givest thou him?
> Or what receiveth he of thine hand?"

He goes on to show how man's wickedness may be a matter of personal concern to men, for they may in some way suffer from it; but one look at the heavens is surely enough to convince any one that God is infinitely above any power of evil which we possess. God's relation to us, then, is not to be regarded as any sort of treaty by which we are bound to do something for his benefit, while he agrees to do certain things for us. He is absolute sovereign; he needs nothing. His attitude toward us is that of a loving master to his servants. Elihu does not reach the idea of a "Father in heaven," but he comes very close to it.

This being the relation of God to men, it seems necessary to answer Job's complaint that oppressed and afflicted innocence gets no answer to its cry. Elihu answers that the mere fact of distress does not give any one a claim on God's help. If they turn their back on God in prosperity, why should he regard the cry that is the mere groan of pain, with neither faith nor repentance in it?

> "They cry for help by reason of the arm of the mighty.
> But none saith, Where is God my Maker,
> Who giveth songs in the night? . . .
> There they cry, but none giveth answer,
> Because of the pride of evil men.
> Surely God will not hear vanity,
> Neither will the Almighty regard it."

The thought here is not unlike that in Proverbs, where Wisdom crieth,

> "Because I have called and ye refused;
> I have stretched out my hand, and no man regarded;
> But ye have set at nought all my counsel,
> And would none of my reproof:
> I also will laugh in the day of your calamity;

> I will mock when your fear cometh;
> When your fear cometh as a storm,
> And your calamity cometh on as a whirlwind;
> When distress and anguish come upon you.
> Then shall they call upon me, but I will not answer."

How often this is true of us in some measure! In our prosperity we forget the goodness of God. We are so filled and satisfied with the good things of the present life that we have no room in our hearts for thoughts of God our Maker, whose we are by creation, and whose laws we are therefore obliged to obey. Even when in times of darkness God delivers us so that our sorrow is turned to singing —"giveth songs in the night"—we soon forget him.

Many ask, with Job, "Why am I so afflicted?" but how few ask in the times of gladness, "Why is the Lord so kind?" Let us learn to say and sing,

> "Ten thousand thousand precious gifts
> My daily thanks employ;
> Nor is the least *a cheerful heart*,
> That tastes those gifts with joy."

Then Elihu goes on from the consideration of Job's case in particular to a broader view of the whole subject:

> "I will fetch my knowledge from afar."

He now asserts that in this broad view it is undoubtedly true that God does give prosperity to the good and does destroy the evil:

> "If they hearken and serve him,
> They shall spend their days in prosperity,
> And their years in pleasures.
> But if they hearken not,
> They shall perish by the sword."

Finally, he exhorts Job to consider the greatness of God, his unsearchable wisdom:

> "Remember that thou magnify his work,
> Whereof men have sung. . . .
> Behold, God is great, we know him not;
> The number of his years is unsearchable."

Then he goes on with another of the sublime hymns in which the book abounds:

THE HYMN OF THE RAIN.

> "For he draweth up the drops of water,
> Which distil in rain from his vapor;
> Which the skies pour down
> And drop upon man abundantly.
> Yea, can any understand the spreading of the clouds,
> The thunderings of his pavilion?
> Behold, he spreadeth his light around him;
> And he covereth the bottom of the sea.
> For by these he judgeth the peoples;

He giveth meat in abundance.
He covereth his hands with the lightning,
And giveth it a charge that it strike the mark.
The noise thereof telleth concerning him,
The cattle also concerning the storm that cometh up.
At this also my heart trembleth,
And is moved out of its place.
Hearken ye unto the noise of his voice,
And the sound that goeth out of his mouth.
He sendeth it forth under the whole heaven,
And his lightning unto the ends of the earth.
After it a voice roareth:
He thundereth with the voice of his majesty;
And he stayeth them not when his voice is heard.
God thundereth marvelously with his voice;
Great things doeth he, which we cannot comprehend.
For he saith to the snow, Fall thou on the earth;
Likewise to the shower of rain,
And to the showers of his mighty rain.
He sealeth up the hand of every man;
That all men whom he hath made may know it.
Then the beasts go into coverts,
And remain in their dens.
Out of the chamber of the south cometh the storm:
And cold out of the north.
By the breath of God ice is given,
And the breadth of the waters is straitened.
Yea, he ladeth the thick cloud with moisture;
He spreadeth abroad the cloud of his lightning;
And it is turned round about by his guidance,
That they may do whatsoever he commandeth them

Upon the face of the habitable world:
Whether it be for correction, or for his land,
Or for mercy, that he cause it to come.
Hearken unto this, O Job:
Stand still, and consider the wondrous works of God.
Dost thou know how God layeth his charge upon them,
And causeth the lightning of his cloud to shine?
Dost thou know the balancings of the clouds,
The wondrous works of him which is perfect in knowledge?"

CHAPTER VIII.

OUT OF THE WHIRLWIND.

"Then the Lord answered Job out of the whirlwind."

HERE is a wonderful answer to prayer. But all answer to prayer is so wonderful that this is perhaps but a little extraordinary. Unusual in manner and wonderfully beautiful in expression, it may perhaps awaken in us some more adequate appreciation of the truth that our God is a prayer-hearing God, and that "the effectual, fervent prayer of a righteous man availeth much." That the desire and petition of a creature like man should at all affect the purpose of the all-wise Creator and Ruler of the world is surely a marvelous thing, not sufficiently regarded. The privilege of prayer, of direct and constant access to the very throne of God, is as amazing as it is sublime. The pool of Bethesda was troubled at certain seasons, and it was believed that whosoever first stepped in after the troubling of the water was made whole of whatsoever disease he had. For this hope a multitude of sick, blind, lame and withered folk lay waiting for the moment when they might scramble for the first touch of the healing waters. But here is a well-spring whence healing and sympathy and blessing flow perennially, not for one, but for all who come.

Job had cried to God with an earnest and distressful cry. He had called on him to speak on his behalf, to vindicate him from the unkind accusations of his friends, or else himself accuse him, that he might know his fault.

It was a cry from the depths. It was the cry of one ready to perish. It was intense and pitiful. Sometimes, indeed, it overstepped the bounds of reverence and became a demand. He almost claims as his right that God should explain his treatment of him, or at least that he should give him a hearing and let him plead his cause before him.

> "Though he slay me, yet will I wait for him:
> Nevertheless I will maintain my ways before him. . . .
> Behold now, I have ordered my cause;
> I know that I am righteous. . . .
> Then call thou, and I will answer;
> Or let me speak, and answer thou me.
> How many are mine iniquities and sins?
> Make me to know my transgression and my sin."

This desire to argue our cause with God is very natural and very common. In our distress how often we demand, as though of right, some explanation of our suffering! We cry bitterly, "Why am I afflicted thus? Why do all these sorrows fall on me more than on others? Must I suffer in the dark, endure and know no reason for it?" Job's cry is the cry of all who suffer, more or less distinctly uttered. Sometimes it is an impious and blasphemous challenge of God's justice; sometimes it is the sobbing of a child who lovingly obeys, but cannot quite keep back the tears of pain and disappointment; sometimes it is the almost inarticulate cry of the great masses of mankind who suffer and are wretched and degraded. They cry with a pitiful cry, as

> "An infant crying in the night,
> An infant crying for the light,
> And with no language but a cry."

The Lord's answer to Job is an answer to all whose cry is, like his, a cry for light. No prayer is disregarded at the throne of Heaven, and no honest, faithful petition fails of an answer. These answers may be given in ways we would not anticipate and by means that look to us both inadequate and irrelevant, but given they always are, somehow and some time. In one of three ways God answers honest prayer:

First, by granting our petitions. This he does more often than we sometimes think, for he does it in times and ways which we do not observe.

Second, by changing our desires, so that we cease to wish for what we asked, seeing that something else is better. The cripple who sat at the beautiful gate of the temple and asked an alms of Peter and John did not get what he asked for, but when he felt his feet and ankle-bones receive strength and realized that he was a sound man, how he leaped and walked and praised God! So in some degree each of us has probably seen some of his petitions refused only to make way for higher gifts. Thus it is a cause of thankfulness that God does not always grant the things we ask as we expect them to be granted.

But, third, he may, and often does, so lift us up above the care and the interests we prayed about that we no longer give them a thought. He answers by "the expulsive power of a new affection." It was after this manner that he answered Job.

When Jehovah speaks, Devotion cries, "Hear, O heavens, and give ear, O earth." Doubt and

Perplexity say, "Now we will know the certainty of things." When we read that the Lord answered Job, we expect an answer to the questions so warmly debated between him and his friends. We feel that they are not yet answered. They have raised questions which neither they nor we have been able to answer.

True, we were taken behind the scenes in the very beginning of the book. We saw the malice of Satan accusing Job of selfishness and insincerity; we saw the high commission of Heaven given to Satan to afflict Job. But our perplexity is rather increased by what we see. Why did God let Satan loose on Job? Why the "perfect and the upright man" should be so afflicted we have received no hint. True, also, we have seen some good effects produced in Job by his sore trials. We have seen in him the heroism of endurance. We have seen a great soul warred against by all the powers of darkness, yet victorious. "Perplexed, yet not unto despair; smitten down, yet not destroyed." A noble spectacle! We have heard the young man's very happy suggestions that affliction is not necessarily an evil. It may be not even correction, but education; the admirable means of developing the noblest and fairest graces.

But all this gives no answer to the question, "What is the exact relation between godliness and prosperity, virtue and happiness?" When we hear that the Lord answered, we listen to have our questions answered and our doubts removed. This is well enough, but not the best way to listen. It is well to ask questions of the Lord, but better simply to say, "Speak, Lord, for thy servant heareth." It is well to know all that may be known of God and his ways of dealing with us, but it is more important to know personal duty. When we seek the former we are frequently disappointed; the finite cannot comprehend the infinite; but when we ask what is present personal duty we are not often left in great perplexity.

If we come to these chapters expecting to have the whole scheme of providence made clear to us, we shall be disappointed. The first thing that strikes us on reading them is that they do not answer the questions that have been so warmly discussed in the book. The whole discourse is general. It has to do with the wisdom of God infinitely transcending the wisdom of man, and the omnipotence of God in contrast with the impotence of man. It makes no reference to Job's case, and very little to his character or conduct. Twice only, and very briefly, he is addressed directly, and each time it is a rebuke. The first is the question,

> "Who is this that darkeneth counsel
> By words without knowledge?"

He is thus called to account for "darkening the counsel" of Jehovah, misinterpreting his works, misrepresenting his designs. God's purposes are like the clear sky, deep, high, boundless, but serene and sublime. Our speculations concerning them are earth-born clouds, thick, murky and depressing. To-day I read an essay* of Mr. Huxley's subtile skepticism. It is keen, shrewd, hard to answer. But I took up the simple narrative of the life of a devoted missionary † of the cross, and the contrast was a striking illustration of the difference between God's work and man's argument. The essay is the logic of a great and well-trained intellect attempting to prove and disprove certain propositions; the latter is the simple record of a noble life and of notable events. The former is full of petty difficulties; the latter is full of great wonders. The former is chiefly questioning "how can these things be?" the latter is the careful record of

* *Nineteenth Century*, July, 1890.
† Rev. John G. Paton of the New Hebrides.

things that *are*, and are more wonderful than all that Mr. Huxley calls in question. The facts of providence and grace which are attested by the missionary are the wonderful, fathomless sky of his eternal purpose; the questions which perplex us about these facts are but the clouds of man's limited apprehension.

This, I take it, is the relation between Job's painful questioning and Jehovah's answer of simple fact—great, unquestioned and unquestionable facts of creation and providence.

These facts are brought forward with wonderful poetic beauty. From a purely literary point of view there is no grander poetry in human language than this

CREATION HYMN.

"Where wast thou when I laid the foundations of the earth?
   Declare if thou hast understanding.
   Who determined the measures thereof, if thou knowest?
   Or who stretched the line upon it?
   Whereupon were the foundations thereof fastened?
   Or who laid the corner-stone thereof;
   When the morning stars sang together,
   And all the sons of God shouted for joy?
   Or who shut up the sea with doors,
   When it brake forth, as if it had issued out of the womb?
   When I made the cloud the garment thereof,
   And thick darkness a swaddling-band for it,

And prescribed for it my decree,
And set bars and doors,
And said, Hitherto shalt thou come, but no further;
And here shall thy proud waves be stayed?
Hast thou commanded the morning since thy days began,
And caused the dayspring to know its place? . . .
Hast thou entered into the springs of the sea?
Or hast thou walked in the recesses of the deep?
Have the gates of death been revealed unto thee?
Or hast thou seen the gates of the shadow of death?
Hast thou comprehended the breadth of the earth?
Declare if thou knowest it all."

Then the theme of the poem flows on from creation to providence, from the making of all things by the word of his power to the most holy, wise and powerful governing of all creatures and all their actions. There is no break in the continuity of the poem, for there is none in the work it celebrates. He who creates, sustains. What are the "resident forces" of nature but the immanence of God's power? What are the laws of nature but the consistent methods of his working? The wind which blows to-day is to us capricious only because we do not know, or know imperfectly, the complicated forces which produce it and direct it. There are no "freaks" of nature, nothing accidental; all is cosmos, beautiful order, for all is the work of the eternal and unchangeable God; "in him we live and move and have our being." The world is not governed *by* law, but *according to* law; that by which all things are governed, that which created and sustains the forces of nature, is to science the great unknown. To this point science brings us, and at this point revelation takes up the theme and adds, " What therefore ye worship in ignorance, this set I forth unto you, The God that made the world and all things therein." He who made, sustains. He who began, continues. *Continuity* is to-day the most emphatic word of natural science, and immanent sovereignty of the unchangeable God is the word of revelation. Are not these two the same? At all events, the hymn of creation passes, without a break, into the

HYMN OF NATURE.

" Where is the way to the dwelling of light,
 And as for darkness, where is the place thereof? . . .
 By what way is the light parted,
 Or the east wind scattered upon the earth?
 Who hath cleft a channel for the water-flood,
 Or a way for the lightning of the thunder;
 To cause it to rain on a land where no man is;
 On the wilderness, wherein there is no man;
 To satisfy the waste and desolate ground;
 And to cause the tender grass to spring forth?

Hath the rain a father?
Or who hath begotten the drops of dew?
Out of whose womb came the ice?
And the hoary frost of heaven, who hath gendered it?
Canst thou bind the cluster of the Pleiades,
Or loose the bands of Orion?
Canst thou lead forth the Mazzaroth in their season?
Or canst thou guide the Bear with her train? . . .
Who hath put wisdom in the dark clouds?
Or who hath given understanding to the meteor? . . .
Wilt thou hunt the prey for the lioness?
Or satisfy the appetite of the young lions,
When they couch in their dens,
And abide in the covert to lie in wait?
Who provideth for the raven his food,
Where his young ones cry unto God,
And wander for lack of meat?"

So the beautiful poem goes on, touching here and there the chords of Nature's boundless harmony, the wild goats of the rock, and the hinds of the open field; the wild ass, "whose house I have made the wilderness, . . . he scorneth the tumult of the city; the wild ox, who cannot be yoked to the furrow;" the ostrich and the eagle, and especially the horse, are cited as wonderful works of God. It is no pale sentimental saint who drew this picture of the horse. It has the ring of genuine and enthusiastic admiration:

"Hast thou given the horse his might?
Hast thou clothed his neck with the quivering mane?
Hast thou made him to leap as a locust?
The glory of his snorting is terrible.
He paweth in the valley, and rejoiceth in his strength:
He goeth out to meet the armed men.
He mocketh at fear, and is not dismayed;
Neither turneth he back from the sword.
The quiver rattleth against him,
The flashing spear and the javelin.
He swalloweth the ground with fierceness and rage:
Neither believeth he that it is the voice of the trumpet.
As oft as the trumpet soundeth he saith, Aha!
And he smelleth the battle afar off,
The thunder of the captains, and the shouting."

In the midst of this sublime song of Nature the Lord addresses Job the second time, saying,

"Shall he that cavileth contend with the Almighty?
He that argueth with God, let him answer it."

But Job is done with caviling. He has been looking up and out upon the wondrous world of God, and when he is suddenly asked to look at himself and his case which he had so loudly cried out about, he can scarcely see it.

"Job answered the Lord, and said, Behold, I am of small account." This is the effect produced on Job by the contemplation of God's power and wisdom as it is revealed in the works of creation and providence. The lurking doubt as to God's justice is gone for ever from the mind of Job. He has no longer any vague, distressing fear that God had overlooked him and was doing him injustice. He is abashed to drag his petty case into the court where the destinies of worlds and solar systems are determined. He is ashamed to remember that he misdoubted the tender care of Him who feeds the raven and satisfies the appetite of the young lion. Job is nowhere greater than when he answered, "Behold, I am of small account;" never more eloquent than when he said, "I lay my hand upon my mouth."

Once more the poet celebrates the wonders of the realm of Nature. He sings, in a style peculiarly Oriental, of the two great monsters of the river: "Behold now behemoth,* which I made with thee," and leviathan,† who is "king over all the sons of pride."

Once more Job answers as before:

"I have uttered that which I understood not;
Things too wonderful for me, which I knew not. . . .
I had heard of thee by the hearing of the ear;
But now mine eye seeth thee:

* The hippopotamus. † The crocodile.

> Wherefore I abhor myself, and repent
> In dust and ashes."

Thus concludes the most beautiful poem in the world. The "perfect and upright man" of the opening chapter has become the man of an humble and contrite heart. The suffering saint who clamored for a hearing of his case has had his wish, but to our surprise he throws up his hand, saying, "Behold, I am of small account." How is this? What has God said to Job thus to transform him? Nothing, except to call his attention to what he could have seen for himself. He explains nothing, argues nothing, alters nothing, yet Job is satisfied by the wonderful works of creation and providence that his God is good and wise, and maketh no mistakes. He is penniless and childless and suffering still; he is without hope of relief or prospect of restoration, but he is at ease and quiet in spirit, for he feels that

> "Underneath are the everlasting arms."

The book of Job ends now with a few brief sentences in prose. These tell us of Job's restoration. The first thing restored is the impaired relation between him and his three friends. They had been very harsh in their judgments and bitter in their accusations, and it would be very hard for Job to feel the same cordial love for them that he felt before. Good friends are the choicest of blessings, and a brother offended is not easily won over to friendship again. The relations here are somewhat strained, and a little irritation is felt in memory of the past. See how the Lord prescribes for such a case:

He makes Job the advocate and intercessor for his three friends. They are commanded to bring a burnt offering for their sin, and Job is asked to pray for them. It is an appeal to his generosity; it touches the great heart of Job. He prays for them with earnest, honest petition. As he prays all bitterness disappears from his own heart. The Lord forgives, and peace and kindliness are thoroughly restored.

But this is not all: Job's restoration to prosperity is connected with this prayer for others. "And the Lord turned the captivity of Job *when he prayed for his friends:* and the Lord gave Job twice as much as he had before."

From grace to grace God leads his saints. The perfect and upright man became the hero of patient faith; then humble and reverent; and at last we see him on his knees in intercessory prayer for those who had tried his patience as few men are ever tried. His discipline is ended. The trial of his faith is perfect. He rises from his knees to be promoted now to greater honor and prosperity. He receives of the Lord's hand double measure. All worldly goods are restored two-fold, and sons and daughters also, for ten grew up about him to comfort his declining years, and ten had gone before to meet him in the heavenly home, when, at length, he died, "being old and full of days."

THE END.

www.ingramcontent.com/pod-product-compliance
Lightning Source LLC
Chambersburg PA
CBHW031333160426
43196CB00007B/677